BIRTH OF A NEW INDIA

[Fresh Light on the Contributions made by Bentinck, Dalhousie and Curzon in the Nineteenth Century]

Suresh Chandra Ghosh

Originals
Delhi-110052

Distributed By :
D. K. Publishers Distributors P Ltd.
4834/24, Ansari Road, Darya Ganj,
New Delhi-110002
Phones : 3278368, 3261465
Fax : 3264368
visit us at : WWW.dkpd.com
e-mail:dkpd@de13.vsnl.net.in

©S.C. Ghosh

First Published 2001

ISBN 81-7536-221-9

Published By :
ORIGINALS
(an imprint of Low Price Publications)
A-6, Nimri Commercial Centre,
Near Ashok Vihar Phase-IV,
Delhi-110052
Phone : 7401672, 7452453
visit us at:www.lppindia. com
e-mail:lpp@nde.vsnl.net.in

Printed At:
D.K. Fine Art Press P. Ltd.
Delhi-110052

PRINTED IN INDIA

For :
Martha Friendenthal-Haase
And Ralf Koerrenz

CONTENTS

Preface

I   Introduction   9

II Bentinck, Macaulay and the Introduction of English Education in India.   17

III Dalhousie, Charles Wood and the Education Despatch of 1854.   32

IV The Utilitarianism of Dalhousie and the Material Improvement of India.   53

V The Genesis of Curzon's University Reform, 1899-1905.   72

Select Bibliography.   121

Index.   127

By the same Author :

1. The Social Condition of the British Community in Bengal 1757-1800 (1971).

2. Dalhousie in India, 1848-56 (1975).

3. The Educational Strategies in the Developing Countries (ed.) (1976)

4. The Peninsula of Gujarat in the Early Nineteenth Century (ed.) (1976).

5. The Development of Educational Service, 1858-79 (Co-ed.) (1977).

6. The Development of the University Education, 1916-20 (ed.) (1977).

7. Indian Nationalism (1985)

8. Educational Policy in India Since Warren Hastings (1986).

9. Freedom Movement in India (1991).

10. The Development of the Educational Service, 1879-96 (ed.) (1991).

11. The History of Education in Modern India, 1757-1986, (1995).

12. The British in Bengal (Indian edition of the work published earlier at Leiden) (1998)

13. The History of Education in Modern India, 1757-1998, (Revised and updated edition of the work published earlier) (2000).

PREFACE

Birth of a New India consists of four articles on Bentinck, Dalhousie and Curzon which appeared in learned journals abroad in the past two decades and a half. Each one of the articles either corrects an error or rediscovers the truth in the specific contribution relating to the creation of a New India and as such they are highly useful and relevant for researchers on Modern India. Since these articles were published abroad, they were not easily accessible to the learned audience in India as very few universities and learned societies in India subscribe to these journals. Three of the four articles form the basis of my lectures delivered to the students at the M.Phil/Ph.d. programme at the Zakir Husain Centre every year but because of their difficult inaccessibility, students face tremendous difficulties in locating them. Once these articles are easily available, say, in a monograph, they will not only enrich the knowledge of our students and scholars but also dispel many a myth such as Macaulay as the harbinger of English education or Wood as the father of the modern education system, which prevails both among the specialist and the non-specialist audience in the country. With that end in view, I have decided to bring them out in a monograph after obtaining the necessary permission from the concerned journals which carried these articles in the past and I shall deem my endeavour highly rewarded if the work meets the appreciation of those for whom it is meant.

JNU, New Delhi   **SURESH C. GHOSH**

Chapter-I

INTRODUCTION

Briton Martin, Jr., has identified the birth of the Indian National Congress in 1885 with the birth of a New India[1] but the creation of this New India is not complete till the first post-natal outbursts of her nascent nationalism as expressed in the protests of educated Indians against Curzon's programme on university reform between 1899 and 1905. The protests of the educated Indians have been overlooked by the historians of the freedom movement who have mostly and largely concentrated on Curzon's act of partitioning Bengal in 1905 as an event of enormous significance giving a shape and direction to our struggle for freedom through the Anti-Partition Movement which followed it. Coming closely in the wake of Curzon's university reform which culminated in the Indian Universities Act of 1904-5, one can argue that the ground for the depth and the extent of the Anti-Partition Movement was largely prepared by the already existing anger and the frustration of the educated Indians against Curzon at his programme on university reform.

While Curzon thus made an indirect contribution through his programme for university reform to the making of a New India, two of his illustrious predecessors in the nineteenth century positively and consciously contributed to it. One of them was Bentinck, the Governor-General of India between 1828 and 1835 and the other was Dalhousie, the Governor-General of India during 1848 and 1856. While Bentinck's administration saw the introduction of English as the official language replacing the Persian[2] to meet the needs and requirements of a growing British administration, Dalhousie's Governor-Generalship saw the crystallisation of the educational experiments carried out by him and by his predecessors into the emergence of a modern educational system in the country. Working under the spell of the utilitarian philosophy of Bentham and Mill, both Bentinck and Dalhousie attempted to improve the tone of the Indian society by stripping it of its various existing social evils such as Sati, infanticide, child marriage and polygamy. However, Dalhousie went further not merely in arguing the case for the spread of education among girls and women but also in introducing three important Western innovations in the form of railways, electric telegraph and uniform postage which were destined to modernise India. While we do not deny the existence of the stark imperial motives behind the introduction of English education and Western technological innovations in the country, there is no doubt that they ultimately benefited the people of India. If the New Education spreading Western political ideas among its recipients coming from diverse geographical regions, races, languages, religions and cultures made them conscious about their rights and privileges, the Western innovations particularly the railways bridging the long distances existing among the different parts of India brought the educated Indians closer together, in their resolve to fight against the British Raj to redress their grievances.

While there had been no personality or event to rob Curzon of his indirect contributions to the making of a New India, such a personality or an event or both existed in the cases of Bentinck and Dalhousie respectively. Bentinck who was cold-shouldered by the Court of Directors for passing an order replacing Persian by the English as the official language, was actually robbed of the credit for it by Macaulay. Macaulay who came to India as the Law Member of Bentinck's Council in June 1834 and was subsequently appointed President of the General Committee of Public Instruction in December of that year wrote that rhetorical minute in February 1835 which seems to have propelled Bentinck to action when he passed that celebrated order next month. And so, all persons in India, both elite and non-elite,, associate the name of Macaulay with the introduction of English education in India. This is partly because of the publicity that Macaulay's Minute of 2 February 1835 received through his brother-in-law, Charles Edward Trevelyan and partly because of his ignorance of, and therefore contempt for, Oriental learning and literature as shown by his several rhetorical utterances in his Minute such as "a single shelf of a good European library was worth the whole native literature of India and Arabia.[3]" It is precisely because of such observations that Macaulay's name and his minute were used by the militant nationalist leaders to whip up anti-British sentiments among the Indians during the freedom struggle. What's more, even today we are used to cursing Macaulay whenever something goes wrong with the English education in the country.

However, Dalhousie's fate was worse than Bentinck's— not only because of a historical person but also because of a historical event. While the historical person was Charles Wood, the President of the Board of Control set up in 1773 to supervise the activities of the Court of Directors, the executive body of the East India Company, the historical event was the Revolt of 1857 which ended the rule of the East India Company in India. Charles Wood was requested by the Court of Directors during the course of the debates in Parliament on the eve of the renewal of the Company's Charter Act in 1853 to draw a comprehensive plan for the the education of the people of British India. Wood's Secretary Northbrook drew up a plan for education based not only on the materials supplied by Dalhousie but also on the latter's educational experiments in British India. However, Wood made a conscious attempt to deprive Dalhousie of his contributions to the making of the plan for education by omitting his name from the list of persons who had helped Wood in its preparation but also took the whole credit for it by boasting in a letter to Colville, Dalhousie's Legislative Councillor and Law Commissioner : "I hope to have laid the foundation of a great improvement in the condition of the natives of our Indian territories."[4] Wood was not one of the signatories to the Education Despatch of 1854 which carried to British India the plan for education—yet such was the force of publicity accorded to the Court of Director's request to him to draw a plan for education that the Education Despatch of 1854 is known in India among the educationists as the Wood's Despatch. And nothing can be more farther from the truth than this description of the Education Despatch of 1854 as the Wood's Despatch!

Dalhousie was not only deprived of the credit for his contribution to the making of the Education Despatch of 1854 but also had to bear the blame and responsibility for the out-break of 1857 which shook the East India Company and ultimately replaced it by the British Crown. He died a lonely and crippled man within a couple of years of this event. Nobody then realised the extent of his contributions to the making of a New India. He not only endorsed the social reforms of one of his illustrious predecessors, Bentinck, but added to them.

He talked of effecting a "social revolution" when called upon to deal with the problem of female infanticide in the newly acquired territories in the Punjab. He noted how the degradation of Indian women was tenaciously adhered to by the Hindus and the Muslims and felt that it was education alone among women which could civilise the body of Indian society. He was the first Governor-General to provide official support to female education in India as "no single change in the habits of the people" was "likely to lead to more important and beneficial consequences than the introduction of education for their female children."[5] He drafted the bill for the remarriage of the widows on the eve of his departure from India, which became an Act under his successor, Canning. There is no doubt that the introduction of Western innovations—railways, electric telegraph and the uniform postage—tightened the imperialist grip over British India but at the same time they became, as he described them in his final minute, "the three great engines of social improvement."[6] While they brought different parts of British India inhabited by people of different races, cultures, religions and languages closer to each other, his railways dealt severe blows at the cast-ridden Indian society when a Brahmin travelled with a Shudra—a mere touch of him was to loose one's caste—as a co-passenger in a railway compartment. In this context we can hardly resist the temptation to quote below the judgement passed by Arnold, a contemporary of Dalhousie, on the impact of the railways, shortly after its introduction into India :

"The real work of the steam-engine in India is yet to be manifested. Those who have travelled on an Indian line, or loitered at a Hindoo railway station, have seen the most persuasive missionary at work that ever preached in the East. Thirty miles an hour is fatal to the slow deities of paganism, and a pilgrimage done by steam causes other thoughts to arise at the shrine of Parvati or Shiva than the Vedas and Shastras inculcate. The Hindoo sees many villages and hills now beside his own; he travels, that is, he learns, compares, considers and changes his ideas. Railways may do for India what dynasties have never done— what the genius of Akbar the Magnificent could not effect by Government nor the cruelty of Tipoo Sahib by *Violence*; they make India a nation."[7]

We now come back to Curzon. We have said at the beginning that the birth of a New India was not complete without the first post-natal protests organised by the educated Indians against Curzon's university reform. The reason why Curzon launched on a programme of university reform was to stop the five universities at Calcutta, Bombay, Madras, Lahore and Allahabad in India turning out, in the words of Curzon "only a discontented horde of office seekers, whom we have educated for places which are not in existence for them to fill."[8] The educated Indians had imbibed from the higher education a tone of mind and a type of character that was "ill-regulated, averse from discipline, discontented, and in some cases actually disloyal."[9] However, the educated Indians could easily see through his motives and organised a "fierce agitation" not only in Bengal, but also in Bombay and Madras against Curzon's programme of university reform. These protests not only demonstrated for the first time a solidarity among the educated Indians for a cause, that is, higher education, which "lies" as Surendra Nath Banerjea pointed out at the Ahmedabad Session of the Indian National Congress in December 1902, "at the root of all our progress"[10] but also the strength and stamina of a New India that was born in 1885. The protests of the educated Indians against Curzon's university reform, which took the shape of a "fierce agitation" in the words of Curzon, were the first organised protests by the Indian National Congress after its birth and prepared the ground for a greater, deeper and wider movement that was soon to engulf the country when Curzon partitioned Bengal in 1905.

*   *   *

Based on archival and other sources at Edinburgh London, Nottingham, Calcutta and Delhi, the four articles in the work attempt to put the contributions of the three Governor-Generals—Bentinck, Dalhousie and Curzon—in correct perspective. Thus in the first article we have shown how the credit for introducing English education in the country should rest not with Macaulay, as universally believed, but with Bentinck. Similarly in the second article we have emphasised Dalhousie's contributions to the making of the Education Despatch of 1854, implementation of which led to the foundation of a modern educational system in India while the third one highlights the ideas behind Dalhousie's endeavour in modernising India against his popular image of an imperialist ruler responsible for the Revolt of 1857. And finally in the last article we have shown that the genesis of Curzon's university reform of 1899-1905 lay not so much in his attempt to improve the quality and standard of higher education in the country as announced by Curzon himself but in his design to bring it under effective governmental control to check the number of educated Indians who remained unemployed spreading discontent and hostility against the British Raj.

As stated in the preface, each one of the four articles has appeared earlier in a learned journal abroad but because of the difficult inaccessibility of these journals in India, the contents of these articles delineating the contributions of Bentinck, Dalhousie and Curzon to the emergence of a New India remain largely unknown. It is hoped that the articles, taken together, will be able to fill a gap in our knowledge on Modern India.

REFERENCES

1. See Briton, Martin, Jr., *New India, 1885* for details.

2. Persian was the official language of a Muslim administration in Medieval India for more than six hundred years.

3. For Details about Macaulay's Minute on 2 February 1835, See H. Sharp, ed., *Selections from Educational Records of the Government of India,* vol.I, pp. 107-117.

4. Wood to Colvile, 24 October 1854. Wood Papers. India Board Letter Book, Vol.6, p. 119.

5. Government of India to Government of Bengal, 11 April 1850. J.Richey ed., *Selections from Educational Records* Vol.2, p. 59.

6. *Parliamentary Papers* (Houes of Commons), 1856, Vol.45, 245, p.16, para 24.

7. E.Arnold. *The Marquis of Dalhousie's Administration of British India,* Vol.2, pp. 241-42.

8. *University of Calcutta Convocation Addresses,* Vol.3, pp. 841-47.

9. *Home Education A Progs.,* October 1901, No. 19, Appendix A, p. 12.

10. *Report of the Proceedings of the Eighteen Indian National Congress* at Ahmedabad on 23 December 1902, pp. 18-20.

Chapter-II

BENTINCK, MACAULAY AND THE INTRODUCTION OF ENGLISH EDUCATION IN INDIA*

In India Thomas Babington Macaulay is fully credited with the introduction of English education officially, though the necessary order on the subject was issued by Bentinck, the Governor-General of India on 7 March 1835 after going through a long rhetorical minute written by the former on 2 February 1835 at the latter's request. The main themes of Macaulay's minute were : (a) English should replace Persian as the official language; (b) English should be introduced as the medium of instruction in all the institutions of learning as "that language has ready access to all the vast intellectual wealth which all the wisest nations of the earth have created and hoarded in the course of ninety generations"; (c) translation of Western knowledge into vernaculars at that time not properly developed would not be efficacious. On the other hand, Indians well acquainted with Western knowledge and science would have "the inclination and the ability to exhibit European knowledge in the vernacular dialects" and would help "raise up a good vernacular literature in the country" within twenty years. (d) Indians taught through the medium of English would take care of the education of their own countrymen. They would become "a class of persons, Indian in blood and colour, but English in taste, in opinions, in morals and intellect." Finally Macaulay observed, "The languages of

*   Appeared in *History of Education,* London, 1995, Vol.24, No. 1, pp. 17-24

Western Europe civilized Russia. I cannot doubt that they
will do for the Hindoo what they have done for the tartar.''[1]
Thus according to Macaulay, the sole purpose of the introduction of English education in India would not be merely
an indoctrination of Indians through text books and cur-
ricula for subordinate positions in the establishments of the
East India Comapany but to achieve a cultural transmission
among the educated Indians. Few are aware of the fact that
nearly forty-three years before Macaulay's minute on 2
February 1835, an official of the East India Company expressed similar views on the subject when the Company
was yet to become an imperial power and that many years
before the coming of Macaulay to Calcutta in December
1834, Bentinck had not only been keeping in his cupboard
a skeleton of the order which he was to issue on the subject
of English education on 7 March 1835 but also had been
steadily pursuing a policy of gradual introduction of English
education in India since 1829.

II

Let us first of all come to the East India Company
official who anticipated Macaulay many years before his
coming to Calcutta as the Law Member of the Governor-
General's Council. He was Charles Grant. Grant had come
to India in 1767, acquired an immense fortune in the hey
days of plunder and loot following the battles of Plassey
1757 and Buxar (1765)[2] and led a hectic and extravagant
life till 1786 when through family mishaps and close contact
with David Brown, one of the Company's Chaplains and
George Udny of the Company's Civil Service, a great change
came over him.[3] In 1790 he returned home and two years
later completed his first draft of his treatise : ''Observations on the State of Society among the Asiatic Subjects
of Great Britain, particularly in the respect to Morals and
on the Means of improving it.'' In his treatise, Grant charged
the Hindus with dishonesty, corruption, fraud, mutual hatred
and distrust and described their customs such as *Sati* as

barbarous, the Muslims with haughtiness, perfidy, licen-
tiousness and lawlessness and asserted that the intercourse
of the two communities had led to the further debasement
of both because each had imbibed the vices of the other.
Grant blamed the East India Company for viewing those
grave evils with apathy and contended that it was under no
obligation to protect the creed of the Hindus, which was
monstrous and ''subversive of the first principles of reason,
morality and religion.'' As a remedy to all these evils, Grant
suggested a ''healing principle''. namely the supercession
of the existing religions by Christianity through the dissemination of the sciences and literatures of Europe, ''a key
which would at once open a world of new ideas'' to them.

Grant stated that the long intercourse between the
Indians and the Europeans in Bengal rendered it feasible
to use the English language as the medium of instruction.
Moreover, he said, a knowledge of the English language
would immediately place the whole range of European
knowledge within their reach, while translation of English
books into the Indian languages would take a long time and
would be less efficacious. Grant also urged the substitution
of English for Persian as the official language because that
would induce the Indians to learn it. He urged the establishment of English schools under teachers ''of good moral
characater'' hoping that very soon the pupils taught in those
schools would themselves become the teachers of English
to their countrymen. In conclusion, he triumphantly asserted
''the true cure of darkness is light. The Hindus err because
they are ignorant and their errors have never been fairly
laid before them.'' Five years after Grant had made these
''observations'', he published them in the form of a book
in 1797 in London.[4]

When we analyse Grant's observations, the following
points become clear. First Grant wanted replacement of
Persian by English as the official language. Secondly, Grant
wanted to introduce English as the medium of instruction

and was against the translation of English books into Indian languages. Finally young Indians trained in these schools would later take care of the education of their own countrymen. We already know from a brief reference to the main themes of Macaulay's minute of 2 February 1835 that these were also the points highlighted by him while stating the case for the official introduction of English education in India. The question that now may be asked : Was Macaulay aware of Grant's *Observations?*

We do not have any direct evidences on the basis of which we can assert that Macaulay was fully conversant with them. Macaulay was the son of Zachary Macaulay, Governor of a British colony, Sierra Leone. Zachary Macaulay was a member of the Clapham Sect which included such persons as Milner of Queen's College or Simeon of King's College, Cambridge, William Wilberforce, Henry Thronton, James Stephen. They were followers of Jeremy Bentham and David Hume, the Utilitarian Philosophers[5] and many among them like Wilberforce and Grant were also members of the British Parliament. In those days Grant's book as well as James Mill's *History of British India*[6] were often mentioned whenever there had been a debate on the East India Company's affairs in India and for an erudite person like Thomas Babington Macaulay who also later became a member of the Parliament, it is difficult to believe that he did not know either the existence or the themes of Grant's book.

Grant had wanted to civilise the Indian society by diffusing European civilisation through the introduction of European knowledge and science. One year before he came out to India, Macaulay gave a speech to the British Parliament on 10 July 1833 on the occasion of the renewal of the East India Company's Charter which clearly indicated his indebtedness to Grant's *Observations*. In that Parliamentary speech, Macaulay's triumphant rhetoric gave to nineteenth century British imperialism the halo of political altruism, to which he added a cultural sentiment—the greatness and glory of the renascent British nation. Macaulay observed : ''It is scarcely possible to calculate the benefits which we might derive from the diffusion of European civilization among the vast population of the East. What is power worth if it is founded on vice, on ignorance and on misery; if we can hold it only by violating the most sacred duties which as governors we owe to the governed, and which, as a people blessed with far more than ordinary measure of political liberty and of intellectual light, we owe to a race debased by three thousand years of despotism and priest craft?''[7]

The admonishing tone in Macaulay's Parliamentary speech of 1833 could well be compared with the tone with which Grant in 1792 accused the East India Company of viewing the evils of the Indian society with apathy.

III

Macaulay came to India in June 1834 as the Law-Member of the Governor-General's Council. He spent the first seven months of his stay in India at Ooty, a hill station near Madras where the Governor-General of India was also camping since June 1834.[8] In December 1834 Macaulay came to Calcutta and joined his post as Law-Member of the Governor General's Council. In another December, many years ago in 1827, Bentinck was nominated as the Governor-General of the Company's possessions in India. What was exactly the nature of the Company's policy towards education of the people of India at that time?

By the time Bentinck came to India in July 1828, there was indeed a tremendous interest among the Indians of the metropolitan cities of British India to learn English. While enlightened Indians like Raja Rammohan Roy saw in English education an opportunity to deliver his countrymen from obsecurantism and barbarous superstitions, the majority of young Indians saw in it an opportunity to gain employment in various British establishments, officials as well as non-official, that were then emerging in metropolitan cities such as Calcutta, Bombay and Madras and up-country in British India. However, the official position of the East India Company was different from this trend. Education at Calcutta, the headquarters of the East India Company in India, was looked after by a General Committee of Public Instruction which acted in strict interpretation of the Clause 43 of the Charter Act of 1813 providing for the education of the people of India. As per this Clause "a sum of not less than one lac of rupees" in each year out of "the surplus territorial revenues" was to be spent on the revival and improvement of literature and the encouragement of the learned natives of India and on the introduction and promotion of a knowledge of the sciences among the inhabitants of the British territories in India.[9] There was no mention of the introduction of English education in the Clause and though the debates in the both Houses of Parliament meant by "sciences" "Western sciences", the Committee dominated by persons with great admiration for Sanskrit and Arabic literature simply ignored it and began to spend the amount on the revival of Oriental learning and institutions as well as on the encouragement of learned Indians.

Soon the work of the General Committee of Public Instruction encountered stiff opposition from the forces which were then emerging in England and India. In 1817 James Mill, faithfull lieutenant of Jeremy Bentham, published his *History of British India* where he suggested reform of the Indian society which he considered to be static and stagnant on the Benthamite principles and pointed out the key to the progress lay in the introduction of Western science and knowledge. The work obtained for Mill not only his reputation as a historian but also an appointment in the East India House as well as of his more famous son, John Stuart Mill, which led to the establishment of utilitarian influence there on Indian affairs.[10] Secondly, in India a certain section of educated and liberally minded Indians, through their long intercourse with the Europeans in the metropolitan cities had realised the futility of pursuing a system of exclusively classical education and the great possibliities which a knowledge of the language and litera-ture of the West afforded. Their lead was taken by Raja Rammohan Roy who had been instrumental in 1815 drawing up a plan for an English institution at Calcutta[11], the capital of British India till 1911.

While in December 1823 Rammohan Roy opposed the Committee's proposal to establish a Sanskrit College at Calcutta[12], in February 1824, in a strongly worded despatch which bore Mill's stamp, the Court of Directors condemned the Committee's work as "fundamentally erroneous" and impressed upon the members that "the great end should not have been to teach; Hindu learning, but useful learning."[13] Within the Committee itself, the new members who replaced the retired and the dead were imbued with the utilitarian philosophy and they began to oppose the work of the Committee so much so that there were often "recurring and inconvenient" discussions at meetings without any decisions.

For the first few years of Bentinck's Governor-Generalship, this deadlock in education continued but mat-ters came to a head when there was a proposal in early 1833 to reorganise the Agra College on the model of the Hindu College at Calcutta and another next year in April 1834 to convert the Calcutta Madrassa into an institution of Western learning.[14] The acrimonius debates on these proposals led to a discussion of the future education policy of the Company in India and the Committee, by now sharply divided into two opposing camps, Anglicists and Orientalists, decided to send all the papers representing the views of both the camps, to the Governor-General Bentinck for a decision, in January 1835.

As we have already said that by December 1834 Macaulay had become the Law Member of the Governor-General's Council. And by December 1834 also he was appointed President of the General Committee of Public Instruction by the Governor-General for his known erudition and intellectual attainments. As President of the Committee, Macaulay did not participate in the debates but when Bentinck asked him to give his views on the subject, he recorded on 2 February 1835 a long rhetorical minute strongly stating the case for the introduction of English education in India and holding out a threat to resign if his recommendations were not accepted.[15]

And Bentinck gave his "entire concurrence" to them and issued within five weeks of Macaulay's minute the following order on the subject on 7 March 1835:

"His Lordship-in-Council is of opinion that the great object of the British Government ought to be the promotion of European literature and science among the natives of India, and that all funds appropriated for the purpose of education would be best employed on English education alone...

His Lordship-in-Council directs that all the funds which these reforms will leave at the disposal of the Committee, be henceforth employed in imparting to the Native population knowledge of English literature and science through the medium of the English language."[16]

It was this order, and not Macaulay's minute, which marked the beginning of the use of English as the official language replacing Persian in all governmental works in British India.

IV

According to the rules of the East India Company the Governor-General in India could not initiate any important action without first obtaining the approval of its executive body, the Court of Directors in London.[17] Since Bentinck took the decision within a few weeks after receiving the papers from the General Committee of Public Instruction, it was clear that the Governor-General did not have the necessary time to obtain the required sanction of the Court of Directors in those days of steamship navigation, when a despatch from Calcutta used to take not less than three months to reach London. This simple fact does not need the scholarship of a Spear[18] or a Ballhatchet[19] to prove or disprove that Bentinck acted without the authority of the East India Company in London. Writing on the subject more than a hundred years later in *'The Education of India'* Arthur Mayhew argued that Bentinck took the decision without reading Macaulay's minute and was solely motivated by Macaulay's threat to resign.[20] Such argument is contrary to the image of Bentinck that has emerged through recent researches as a true child of his age.

Bentinck who came to India as the Governor-General in July 1828 was a firm believer in utilitarian principles. In a farewell dinner at Grote's house in December 1827 just on the eve of his departure for India, he had said to James Mill: ''I am going to British India but I shall not be Governor-General. It is you that will be Governor-General.''[21] A man of great energy, vigour and action, he utilised the long period of peace enjoyed by his government in tackling every problem that his administration faced in India—he was the person who made *Sati*[22] illegal in 1829 and took steps to stop other social evils like *Thugi* and infanticide.[23] He believed that it was English education alone which could cure the Indian society of its various evils. In a letter to Metcalfe in September 1829 he described ''the British language'' [sic] as ''the key of all improvements''.[24] Acting on his firm belief he took every step of making a wide use of the English language in official works as well as of persuading the young Indians to learn English by throwing open subordinate positions in judicial and revenue branches to the English educated among them though mainly as a measure of economy[25]. In a letter to the General Committee of Public Instruction on 26 June 1829 he observed: "It is the wish and admitted policy of the British Government to render its own language gradually and eventually the languages of public business throughout the country, and that it will omit no opportunity of giving every reasonable and practical degree of encouragement to the execution of this project."[26] As a respect to the wishes of the Governor-General, the General Committee of Public Instruction added English classes to the Benares Sanskrit College in 1830 thereby providing for English classes in all the important Oriental institutions at Calcutta, Delhi and Benares.

A gradual replacement of Persian by English in all official works as well as the spread of English language in educational institutions—these were the twin objects that Bentinck kept before him from the very beginning of his term as the Governor-General of India. His official position did not allow him to support the evangelists in India directly but he was sympathetic to those missionaries who took utmost care in the use of English in their educational institutions. He helped Alexander Duff, the Scottish missionary, to set up his General Assembly's Institution at Calcutta in 1830 which later grew to the still existing Scottish Church College. In "a private interview" given to Alexander Duff in February 1833, Bentinck "heartily approved of the design of giving a higher education to a select few, in preference to the plan of giving a common education to the many."[27] He told Duff that "if there was one opinion on which he was more decided than another, it was the expediency of teaching English in all our Higher Seminaries gradually substituting it throughout every department of government business, instead of the Persian which ought as soon as possible to be abolished."[28]

One important reason why Bentinck was so keen on introducing English education becasue he considered it not only to be a "cure" for the kind of social evils that he had to deal with at the very beginning of his administration in

India but also a key for the improvement of the country. In this respect he fully shared with James Mill the view that the Indian society was decadent and the key to its regeneration lay in the introduction of Western knowledge and science. In a letter to Mancy on 1 June 1834, he explained: "General education is my panacea for the regeneration of India. The ground must be prepared and the jungle cleared away before the human mind can receive, with any prospect of *real* benefit, the seeds of improvement... You wil anticipate my entire dissent from those who think it better that the natives should remain in ignorance. I cannot regard the advantage of ignorance to the governors or the governed. If our rule is bad, as I believe it to be let the natives have the means through knowledge, to represent their grievances and to obtain redress. If their own habits, morals or way of thinking are inconsistent with their own happiness and improvement, let them have the means provided by our greater intelligence of discovering their errors. I approve therefore of every plan by which the human mind can be instructed and of course elevated..."[29]

Such a plan came through Macaulay's minute of 2 February 1835 as an expert advice on the subject and Bentinck immediately acted on it. Macaulay, whose interest in consolidating the British empire by the propogation of English laws and English culture began quite early in life when he grew up as the son of Zachary Macaulay in the circle of the Clapham evangelists, held similar views on the subject with Bentinck. And it will not be unreasonable to surmise that there had been earlier discussions on it either at the time when they were together in Ootacamund in the Nilgiris in the summer of 1834 or at the time when Macaulay was appointed by Bentinck as President of the General Committee of Public Instruction in December 1834 at a time when the Committee was seized with the controversy on the future education policy of India. Assuming there had been no such occasions, it was still possible for Macaulay to know the Governor-General's mind through C.E.

Trevelyan, a staunch Anglicist and the most favourite among Bentinck's officials, who married Macaulay's sister.[30] The threat of resignation held out by Macaulay if his recommendations on English education were not accepted was not a threat meant for Bentinck but a subtle challenge thrown to the opponents of English education in India.

The reason why Bentinck issued the order without obtaining the approval of the Court of Directors was because of the fact that following return of the Tory Party to power in England Bentinck was contemplating his retirement as the Governor-General of India by the end of March 1835.[31] He did not want to leave the fate of a subject so dear to his heart to his successor and took immediate steps to decide on it on 7 March 1835. And he did so at a price— he earned the displeasure of the Court of Directors to such an extent that back home he withdrew himself from the affairs of the Company and led a secluded life. The Court of Directors on the other hand almost decided to reverse the order of 7 March 1835 by sending a despatch to Calcutta—the draft of the despatch was almost ready by October 1836 but was never sent as Hobhouse, the President of the Board of Control, did not agree to the draft despatch sent to him by Carnac, Chairman of the Court of Directors, under pressure from Auckland, the Governor-General of India.[32]

Macaulay's minute became a secretarial sensation from the very moment of its composition on 2 February 1835—it shot him to further prominence in England and in India. Within four years large portions of the minute were made public by the zeal of Macaulay's brother-in-law, Charles Trevelyan and within hundred years, that is by 1935, it had been published either in full or in part on nine different occasions. The already great reputation of Macaulay assured the minute's notoriety in India,[33] and later his meridian fame secured its cordial reception in England. We must howerver remember that the minute did not initiate any new policy though it signalled the advance of a policy already pursued by Bentinck since 1829. It gave to Bentinck the confidence to go forward on a subject upon which he lacked the necessary intellectual, though certainly not the moral, conviction. Bentinck's order of 7 March 1835 not only opened Europe to India but India to Europe and signalled the advent of far reaching socio-economic and political changes in India in a none too distant future.

REFERENCES

1. For details about Macaulay's minute on 2 February 1835, see H. Sharp (ed.), *Selections from Educational Records of the Government of India* (Calcutta, 1920), 1, pp. 107-117.

2. Richard Barwell who later became a member of the Governor's Council in Bengal could write to his father from Malda in 1765 : "India is a sure path to competency. A moderate share of attention and your being not quite an idiot are ample qualities for the attainment of riches".

3. The best biographical account of Charles Grant in India is by A.T. Embree, *Charles Grant and British Rule in India* (London, 1962).

4. The manuscript of Grant's *Observations* can be seen at the India Office Library, London as *Mss. Eur E-93.*

5. Asa Briggs, *The Age of Improvement* (London,1946), P. 69.

6. Professor Eric Stokes incorrectly states in his preface to *English Utilitarians and India* (Oxford, 1959) that James Mill undertook his *History of British India* in 1808 and finished it in 1819. In fact he undertook the work before 1808 and published it at London in 3 vols. In 1817. The British Museum possesses a copy of this publication in 1817.

7. Quoted in G.M. Young, ed., *Macaulay, Prose and Poetry* (London, 1967), pp. 717-18.

8. Ooty was a familiar summer resort for Bentinck as it had been known to him since 1807 when he went to Madras as its Governor. For details about, Bentinck's governorship of Madras where he was instructed by the British Foreign Secretary,

Wellesley, to found "British greatness upon Indian happiness", see John Rosselli, *Lord William Bentinck : The Making of a Liberal Imperialist 1774-1839,* (Delhi, 1974), pp. 123-146.

9. Sharp (ed.), *op.cit,* p. 22

10. For a general appraisal of Mill's views on administration, see John Stuart Mill, *Essays on Politics and Culture* edited by G. Himmelfarlo (New York, 1963)

11. The School was set up in 1817 though Roy had to withdrew at the later stage because of the opposition of the conservative group headed by Raja Radha Kanta Deb to his religious views. A. Howell observes in his *Education in British India prior to 1854 and in 1870* (Calcutta, 1872) "the foundation of this college marks an improtant era in the history of education in India, the first spontaneous desire manifested by the natives in the country for instruction in English and the literature of Europe." See p.9.

12. For Roy's letter, see Sharp, ed., *op. cit.,* p.98 *et.seq.* The best biographical work on Rammohan Roy which still holds the field, despite the appearance of many similar. works on the subject, is by Sophia Dobson Collect, *Life and Letters of Raja Ram Mohan Roy* (London, 1900).

13. *Ibid.,* p.91 *et. seq.*

14. *Ibid.,* p.104 *et. seq.*

15. *Ibid.,* p.107 *et. seq.*

16. *Ibid.,* pp.130-01.

17. For details about the organisation of East India Company, see P. Auber, *An Analysis of the Constitution of the East India Company* (London, 1826) and C.H. Philips, *The East India Company, 1784-1834* (Manchester, 1940).

18. T.G.P. Spear, "Bentinck and Education" in the *Cambridge Historical Journal* (Cambridge, 1938-40), VI, 1-3, pp. 78-101.

19. K.A. Ballhatchet, "The Home Government and Bentinck's Education Policy" in *Ibid.* (1950-52), X, 1-3, pp. 224-29.

20. A. Mayhew, *The Education of India* (London, 1925), p.18.

21. Quoted in J. Bowring, ed., *The Works of Jeremy Bentham* (London, 1843), X, pp. 576-77.

22. Self-immolation of a widow on the funeral pyre of her husband. For details, see Edward Thompson, *Sutte* (London, 1928).

23. Sacrifice of a girl child immediately after her birth. See R.W. More, *Hindu Infanticide* (London, 1860) for details.

24. Bentinck to Metcalfe, 16 September 1829. *Bentinck Papers* at the Department of Manuscripts, Nottingham University Library. Microfilm copies of *Bentinck Papers* are now available with the National Archives of India, New Delhi.

25. This economic factor as a motivation to many of Bentinck's administrative measures has been highlighted by Rosselli in his work on Bentinck. See Rosselli, *op. cit.,* p.214.

26. Stirling to the General Committee of Public Instruction, 26 June 1829. *Board's Collections,* 1170, ff. 377-93, at the India Office Library, London.

27. Duff to Inglis, I March 1833. *Duff Papers* at the National Library of Scotland, Edinburgh, M.S. 7530, p.140.

28. *Ibid.*

29. Bentinck to Mancy, I June 1834. *Bentinck Papers* 2643/i.

30. C.E. Trevelyan, a seasoned young administrator who enjoyed Bentinck's trust and affections said succinctly : "What Greek and Latin were to the contemporaries of More and Ascham, our tongue is to the people of India." C.E. Trevelyan, *On the Education of the people of India* (London, 1838), p.43.

31. Charles Metcalfe who later went to Canada as the Governor-General was appointed Bentinck's successor for a year after his retirement on 31 March 1835.

32. For detalis, see K.A. Ballhatchet, "The Home Government and Bentinck's Educational Policy" in the *Cambridge Historical Journal, op.* cit., p.226, *et. seq.*

33. During the struggle for freedom in India, Macaulay's summary rejection and condemnation of Indian history, culture and civilisation in his minute on 2 February 1835 was used by the militant nationalist leaders to whip up anti-Raj feelings among the Indians.

Chapter-III

DALHOUSIE, CHARLES WOOD AND THE EDUCATION DESPATCH OF 1854*

The foundation of a modern educational system in India which has successfully stood the test of time[1] was laid by the Education Despatch of 1854, sent by Charles Wood, the President of the Board of Control, to Dalhousie, the Governor-General of India. The Despatch, also popularly known as the Wood's Education Despatch, was mainly the work of Dalhousie, who supplied Wood with all the necessary materials needed for framing it. Unfortunately Dalhousie's contribution to the making of the Education Despatch was not officially mentioned by Wood and this forms the ground on which scholars who have later worked on the Dalhousie era have rejected Dalhousie's claim for a share in the making of it. And the most important of them is Professor R.J.Moore.

In his article in the *English Historical Review*, Moore has shown how Sir Charles Wood, the President of the Board of Control, and not Dalhousie, the Governor-General of India, had 'planned the Despatch, supervized and helped in the drafting of it with pertinacious care and ultimately admitted or rejected the many suggestions to improve it'.[2] While considering Dalhousie's claim for a share in the composition of the Despatch, he observes :

---

* Appeared in *History of Education*, London, Summer, 1975, Vol.4, No. 2, pp. 37-47

If Wood had made substantial use of letters or documents on education which Dalhousie had sent home, there would be grounds for recognizing claims for the latter's influence upon the Despatch. But this seems scarcely to have been the case.[3]

He reiterates the same view in his *Sir Charles Wood's Indian Policy, 1853-66* :

When wood presented the document to an enthusiastic House of Commons, he listed the names of several men who had coutributed to, or whom he had cousulted about, its contents. Those of Mill and Dalhouse'e were not mentioned. Indeed, the story of Despatch's development may be told without referring to either of them.[4]

The reference to Mill arises from the fact that B.T. McCully in his *English Education and the Origins of Indian Nationalism* has advanced a claim on behalf of John Stuart Mill in connection with the authorship of the Despatch. As he observes:

According to the procedure usual in such matters (of drafting the documents) the initial draft probably was composed at East India House. This would seem to point to John Stuart Mill, who at the time had charge of the political department and in that capacity was alleged to have written almost every 'political' despatch of any importance that conveyed the instruction of the Directors to their pro-consuls in Asia. Mill's interest in the education of the natives lends further strength to the assumption.[5]

McCully himself, however, critically examines the case appertaining to Mill's authorship of the Despatch and comes to the conclusion that 'in the absence of more convincing proof, at least, it would be improper to attribute the language of the Despatch to him'.[6]

But Moor's contention that the story of the Despatch's

development may be told without referring to Dalhousie cannot be justified even by reference to the Wood papers. These papers reveal that Wood was requested by the East India House to frame a general scheme applicable to the whole of India, which could be put in force, with due regard to local circumstances by the government of the several Presidencies,[7] in a proposed PC[8] a practice ultimately leading to the formation of a despatch to India.[9] The occasion for this arose from the discussion which took place in Parliament relating to the Act for the future government of India when great interest was expressed on the subject of education and a strong desire manifested for its extension and improvement.[10] 'With a view to give effect to these feelings and wishes[11] the East India House supplied Wood with all necessary materials for framing a comprehensive policy on education but told him that it would 'not be necessary for the purpose of effecting his important object that the system hitherto acted on, differing greatly as it does in detail in the several Presidencies, should undergo any great or violent change, but rather that the object should be sought by an extension of that system, in some directions, and by the use and encouragement of those Educational Establishments, unconnected with Government, which have found much favour with the general community, but which have hitherto received no countinance or support from the State'.[12] In this connection the East India House particularly recommended to Wood's consideration Thomason's[13] system of vernacular education :

> With regard to the village schools the plan already acted on with success in the NW Provinces and in Bombay assisting and encouraging the efforts of the people themselves for the improvement of existing schools should be adhered to; and there seems [to be] no reason to doubt that this mode of proceeding will be found adequate to the end in view.[14]

Wood's Secretary, later Lord Northbrook, went

through the materials supplied by the East India House carefully and jotted down for him[15] the following main points:

The general result of the information showed that in the North Western Provices alone was there anything approaching to a systematic scheme for educating or improving the education of the people.

That in Bengal and in the neighbourhood of the other Presidency Towns there was a considerable demand for English—which had been responded to by the Government.

That wherever practical education had been attempted it had been most successful and that a very considerable private agency might be taken advantage of, if grants-in-aid were sanctioned.

There was ample information from which to draw up a general scheme—and to make Native Education an integral part of the ordinary administration in India.[16]

The absence of any date and place in 'the various stages through which the Education dft. of 1854 passed'[17] is indeed surprising and perhaps unexpected in the case of one who was, at least in the eyes of his contemporaries, 'a master of detail.[18] This certainly leaves posterity in confusion about the strict chronological development of the different stages in the draft of the Education Despatch. Whatever may be the motives of Wood in such behaviour, the various stages in the draft show that he was well informed by the Court of the East India Company about the development in Indian educational policy with a view to the framing of an education despatch. If Dalhousie had not sent home the necessary papers about educational experiments in India, how could Wood come to know of them from the East India House? In fact, the Education Despatch of 19 July 1854 clearly indicates, on close examination, a borrowing from Dalhousie who was supporting Thomason's scheme for vernacular education on an experimental basis. In paragraph 16 of the Despatch, it refers to Mr. Thomason, the Lt. Governor of Agra, as one who had 'displayed that accurate knowledge of the condition and requirement of the people, under his charge, and the clear and ready perception of the practical measures best suited for their welfare.'[19] The Despatch greatly commended his work in paragraphs 91[20]92[21] and concluded with the following observation in paragraph 93: 'We have already referred to it [Thomason's scheme] as the model by which the effort of other Presidencies... should be guided.'[22] This Dalhousie had proposed to do in 1853, when he decided to extend Thomason's scheme of vernacular education which had proved successful in some districts in the North Western Provinces, to the Punjab and Bengal, long before the coming of the Despatch of 1854. And one may very well agree with a learned contemporary who knew India well, the Boden Professor of Sanskrit in the University of Oxford, Monier Williams:

> One great merit of Mr. Thomason's scheme of popular education was that it contained in itself great aptitude for internal development and improvment. His method was adopted as a model by other Governments, and led in the end to the celebrated educational Despatch from the Court of Directors to the Governor-General of India (Lord Dalhousie) dated July 19th 1854.[23]

A critical study of the Despatch gives the impression that besides adopting Thomason's plan for vernacular education in India, it develops many of Dalhousie's own ideas with regard to techincal and female education in India in paragraphs 31[24] and 83[25] respectively. It also expands Dalhousie's ideas on Indian universities, a model of which he hoped to see in the Presidency College which he had established by reorganizing the Hindu college in 1853.[26] As Wood later admits: 'I am very well pleased to see what you have done as to your Presidency College at Calcutta. It harmonizes very well with our University Scheme.'[27] Again it can be seen in his papers that a few months before the completion of the Despatch he was championing the principle of grants-in-aid to private and missionary schools in India.[28] Dalhousie therefore could easily say: 'The scope of the present despatch from the Honurable Court is more than sufficient to include within its sanction... projects, which have been submitted by the Government of India.'[29] In short, the Education Despatch of 19 July 1854 is not a negation, but an expansion, of the educational policy pursued by Dalhousie and his predecessors in India.

George D. Bearce, who has carefully studied British attitudes towards India from 1784 to 1858, comes to the same conclusion on the basis of a study of other sources:

In most respects there was nothing new in Wood's programme for Indian education. Elements of Wood's comprehensive programme went back to the educational ideas of Munro and Elphinstone, to the continuous work of the missionaries since 1813, and to the utilitarian ideas about education found in Macaulay and James Mill. Attention to technological education—preparing Indians in science and industry for the coming modern world—was a special concern of the age of Dalhousie, for earlier thinkers could hardly visualize the technological education that would accompany railways, irrigation works, and agricultural technology. What was significant about the despatch was its comprehensiveness and the optimism.[30]

Again Kamala Sen, who has studied 'Sir Charles Wood and the Origin and Evolution of Modern University Education in India during the nineteenth century' has shown that the scheme of the modern Indian universities as outlined in Wood's Despatch was not the work of Wood, but of Dr. Mouat, Secretary to the Council of Education in Bengal, who had submitted a similar plan to the Court of Directors through the Government of India for their consideration in 1854. The enthusiasm of Dalhousie and the public opinion in England and India in favour of modern universities in India had much to do with their realization in India.[31]

So by not referring to what the Government of India had done in the field of education and by not acknowledging the various proposals on education submitted to the Court of Directors for their approval before July 1854. Wood had done, as Dalhousie wrote to his most intimate and old friend, Couper, 'the shabbiest injustice to the Government of India'.[32]

Professor Moore has treated the outbrust of such natural sentiments of Dalhousie as evidence that he 'was wont to exaggerate his achievement in the field of vernacular education'.[33] If Moore had studied the Dalhousie Papers besides studying the Wood Papers carefully, if he had studied the Education Despatch of 19 July 1854 critically, and finally if he had made himself acquainted with the educational policy of Dalhousie and his predecessors in India before 1854, he would probably have held a different opinion.

Since the receipt of the request from the Court[34] and the sittings of the Lord's Committee on Education from May to July 1853[35] Wood had been thinking of making some positive steps in the field of education. He had begun to examine witnesses such as Dr. Alexender Duff, the missionary who had initiated the move for better education in India,[36] James Marshman, the editor of the *Friend of India*, Trevelyan and C.H. Cameron.[37] In August he had written to Dalhousie:

> I am also a good deal at sea in education. I have had no time to work into it myself and I don't see anybody who can give me a very unbiased opinion— for I shall be the more obliged to you for enlightening me about it...I should wish you to desire somebody to prepare a report showing existing matters

as they are—and also what is feasible in the way of extension.[38]

In replying in October, Dalhousie told him that for education he would find his complete printed reports of everything for many years past in India House and in the Board Library. They would give him a complete view of education. He also requested him to consult Trevelyan, 'a Pundit upon education and will at once pointed out' what he wanted. And finally he added 'if more is required and you will describe fully what you wish I will endeavour to procure it for you'.[39]

In November 1853 Dalhousie wrote to Wood about 'a very large proposal for native education in the three divisions of the Presidency of Bengal' and other proposals for a General College which were 'on their way through the Government of India'.[40] These proposals were for extending Thomason's system of vernacular education to the rest of the North Western Provinces, Bengal and the Punjab and for the establishment of the Presidency College of Calcutta. He had already written to the Court for their sanction to these proposals. And we know Dalhousie complained officially as he recorded in his Diary after the receipt of the Despatch of 1854 that they had not been acknowledged—not to speak of their sanction to them— even after a lapse of one year.

In a letter of 13 June 1854 he first made this known to Wood a few months before the completion of the Education Despatch. In that letter he pointed out that he had sent home 'a scheme of general vernacular education for all the North Western Provinces' and that its receipt had not yet been acknowledged.[41] Wood gave him no immediate reply to this question.

He repeated his complaint to Wood when he learnt from him that he had sent to India with the sanction of the Home Government 'a draft on education'[42] giving a general scheme for India:

I shall be very happy to receive your despatch on Education. In November 1853 I sent home a proposal for a complete system of Vernacular Education for the NW Provinces, the Punjab and Bengal. The receipt of it has never been acknowledged.[43]

Wood, who had already received Dalhousie's letter of 13 June 1854 where he first heard this complaint wrote to him:

The scheme for vernacular education in NW Provices never came up at the time when you sent it and I only disinterred it from the EI House on the receipt of your letter.[44]

Professor Moore admits that the Company's 'Register of Drafts' gives the date of the receipt of the scheme of Dalhousie as 4 November 1853.[45] This shows that Dalhousie's scheme had certainly arrived at the East India House. Moore has argued that since two months after its arrival, Wood had written to Elphinstone on 24 January that he was 'very anxious' to see Dalhousie's proposed scheme of education, this remark suggests he had seen nothing of it. He has also used his letter of 9 August 1854 to show that since he had seen nothing of Dalhousie's on the question, there seems no reason to question this story'.[46] We know from a study of Wood's Papers that he had been kept well informed about the developments in the field of education in India and he himself had alluded to the successful working of the Thomason's scheme in his papers and hoped this could be a model for any general scheme of education in India. Besides, since the creation of the Board of Control by Pitt's India Act of 1783-4, this body was to exercise a supervisory control over all dealings of the Court of Directors with India.[47] By the mid-nineteenth century the President of the Board of Contol was looked upon as supreme in all Indian affairs. In 1847 Brunnow introduced John Hobhouse, who was then the President of the Board of Control, to the Grand-duke Constantine at one of Lady

Palmerstone's parties: *'C'est le roi des Indes'*.[48] In such an elevated person as the President of the Board of Control, Wood was likely to be in possession of all infromation about India.

It was indeed a very difficult task for one who had no direct acquaintance with the socio-economic life of the country concerned to draw a general plan for education for a vast country like India. In a letter to Marshman, Wood confessed this difficulty: 'I confess that I do not see my way as yet...How we could embark on so gigantic an undertaking.'[49] He had, therefore, to be kept well-informed about educational developments in India and was forced to depend on others directly connected with the educational system in India when compiling the Education Despatch of 1854.[50] In a letter to Dalhousie he named the persons who he had consulted: 'Macaulay, Lord Glenelg, Bayley and Prinsep, Marshman, the Church Missionaries, Berry, Mouatt, Beadon, and everybody we could think of here, as having any authority on the subject, have been consulted, and have cordially approved the scheme.' In the face of this admission it would seem surprising that Wood should take for himself the whole credit for the Education Despatch of 1854. In a letter to Colvile, Dalhousie's Legislative Councillor and Law Commissioner, he boasted: 'I hope to have laid the foundation of a great improvement in the condition of the natives of our Indian territories.'[52] It was quite in keeping with the sentiment of Wood that Dalhousie recorded rather bitterly in his Diary:

> The Education Despatch...is a more clap-trap put forth to the House of Commons by Sir Charles Wood; whereby he seeks to filch for himself the whole credit of all that has been, or is to be done; thus unduly detracting from the credit which fairly belongs to the Government of India and to the local administration.[53]

Wood never told Dalhousie about his plans in the field of education, though he had earlier solicited Dalhousie's help in formulating his ideas. He also consulted many others—and most of them, except Dalhousie the Governor-General of India, had known about the Education Despatch even before it was sent to India.[54] One of them, Marshman, the editor of the *Friend of India*, published 'extracts from the paragraphs' of the Despatch, which he said 'were obtained from the Board of Control and he was so good as to offer a sight of them' to Dalhousie through a gentleman who informed him.[55] But Dalhousie declined, first because he did not wish to let it be supposed that he obtained his first knowledge of a despatch on general education from the *Friend of India* and secondly because he believed that the extracts must be from some draft of an incomplete despatch surreptitiously obtained.[56] After learning from Wood that he had sent the Despatch on 19 July 1854, Dalhousie disclosed this incident to him and added rather sharply:'... I think it right to let you know this, because I feel very sure that it would not have been your wish that this information should reach India thus, and that the confidence of yourself or of your office must have been abused.'[57]

It was Wood's consciousness that Dalhousie was unjustly deprived of a share in the credit for the Education Despatch that led him to make a vain attempt to soothe his feelings:

You seem, as you say, to have fairly done your best as to Education. We have, I think, done ours. We approve all you have proposed—you must execute all that we have directed. I made my statement [in the House of Commons] last night.[58] and the Education Scheme was loudly and proudly approved and we were promised that our names should be handed down together as renovators in India. What prospects of immortality![59]

Posterity, however, would give a better share of credit

to Dalhousie as the 'renovator' of India since Dalhousie was not as narrow in apporach to the educational problems in India as Wood. The Wood Papers show that he was unwilling to provide extensive higher education[60] since this would create a 'discontented class unless they were employed'[61] and would ultimately ruin the British Empire in India. Dalhousie's mind was not haunted by such fear, and given time and opportunity he would have certainly evolved an educational system in India, which with his respect for Oriental learning coupled with his belief in the need for Western knowledge, would probably be practically far superior to what was founded by the Despatch of 1854. The latter, in its introductory paragraphs certainly raised many high hopes and aspirations[62] which were scarcely fulfilled by succeeding Governor-Generals and Viceroys.

Dalhousie, however, did not allow his personal feeling to stand in the way of the implementation of provisions of the Despatch,[63] which opened an era of 'Anglo-Vernacular educational epoch'[64] in the history of Indian education. He realized that 'it contained, a scheme of education for all India, far wider and more comprehensive than the local or the Supreme Governments would have ventured to suggest. It left nothing to be desired.'[65] Its implementation indeed would be 'a tough job', but he assured Wood that he would have 'the cordial exertions of us all'[66] in the determination to put the measures into effect. In execution of the instructions of the Court he sought the assistance of those experienced in educational matters such as the Lt.-Governor of Bengal, Halliday, the Legislative Council Member, Grant and the President of the Council of Education, Colvile.[67]

Dalhousie analysed the subject of the Despatch under three principal heads: (1) Machinery for managing the Department of Education, (2) Establishment of University, and (3) Grants-in-aid, and he proceeded to submit measures under each of them separately. Since, in order to save time, the Court had actually authourized Madras and Bombay to make provisional arrangements, which were to be reported to the Government of India for approval and sanction, his measures were mostly confined to Bengal and the North Western Provinces.

Dalhousie suggested that in each Governorship and Lt.-Governorship an officer should be appointed who was to be called the Director of Public Instruction to supervise the Department of Education. His salary should not exceed Rs.3000 a month but if it was fixed at less than Rs.3000 a month he would be entitled to a gradual increase until it reached that sum so as to retain the services of a competent officer for a considerable time. There should be four Inspectors for Bengal on salaries varying from Rs 500 to Rs.1500 a month and two for the North Western Provinces on salaries of Rs.800 to Rs.1200 a month. The Inspectors were to play an important part in the administration of the Department of Education since the success or failure of the system of grants-in-aid and the well-being of the government and private schools and colleges would depend upon their vigilance and efficiency.

As the Government of Bombay had not yet submitted any scheme, it would be subject to the measure for Bengal and the North Western Provices. Dalhousie also extended this system to Madras which had submitted a different scheme—an Educational Secretary to the Government on a salary of Rs.3333 a month, an Under Secretary and six Inspectors on Rs.1350 a month—in order to introduce uniformity and economy in the administration of the Department of Education.

The next practical step was the Establishment of University. Here Dalhousie noted an ambiguity in the Despatch. Judging from the expressions as well as from the whole purport of the Despatch it could be supposed that the establishment of the university, like all other measures suggested or directed in the document, was to be carried into effect at once by Governor-General-in-Council. More so because the university in its examinations, its connection with and superintendence over affiliated institutions, its power of making rules for the whole (subject to the approval of the Government), and its function of giving degrees, seemed to be almost essential to the vital energy of the new system as laid down in the Despatch. Therefore, the most reasonable and right course to adopt would be to introduce a Bill in the Legislative Council (in analogy with the course pursued in the establishment of London University) to incorporate the university, and also to name and appoint the Chancellor, Vice-Chancellor and Fellows and provide for filling subsequent vacancies in their numbers. But the wording of paragraph 33 in the Despatch precluded him from taking this action. As he said:

> My first impression on receiving the Despatch undoubtedly was, that it was the wish of the Honourable Court that the Goverment of India should proceed to the establishment of the Universities, simultaneously with the other charges which were authorized in the Despatch. The general terms of that document and casual expressions contained in other letters from the Honourable Court still seem to favour that interpretation. It is the one which my own wishes would incline me to adopt, and I am most reluctant to surrender it. But the language of the 33 paragraph is so explicit and precise, it so distinctly requires the Government of India to report in the Honourable Court with reference to the proposed Universities upon the best method of procedure with a view to their incorporation by Acts of the Legislative Council of India, and it differs so markedly from the form of expression employed in Para 20, that I can find no escape from the approach of reporting to the Honourable Court our recommendations respecting the proposed universities before we proceed to give effect to them.[68]

He, therefore, recommended that the Governor-Gen-

eral of Bengal should act provisionally as the Chancellor of
Calcutta University and that the members of his Executive
Council as well as the European and Indian members to the
Council of Education should be its Fellows. He also recommended a list of persons who would constitute 'the
Senatus' and asked the Bombay Government to submit such
a list to him. The Senate of each university should frame
the rules for application for affiliation by the institutions, for
examinations and for the conferring of degrees and honours.
There should be two degrees in each of the subjects, viz.
Literature, Mathematics, Science, Law, Civil Engineering
and Medicine. On the taking of each degree the student
should have, as in London University, an opportunity of
taking honours and those who did not avail themselves of
those opportunities would be tempted by the second degree
to carry their education beyond the low standard of the
common degree as contemplated in the Despatch. It also
suggested the institution of Professorships of Law, Civil
Engineering, the Vernacular and the learned languages of
India. But in Calcutta, since they already existed at the
Hindu College and would be established at the Presidency
College or at the Civil Engineering College, the University
of Calcutta should be, according to the strict model of the
London University, confined to the functions of examining
and giving degrees.

Dalhousie then proceeded to submit measures to carry
out the instructions of the Court relating to grants-in-aid.
The instructions were so sufficient and Dalhousie found
little room for 'much remarks'. The Despatch said that
rules were to be framed for the administration of the grants,
and the framing of these rules would probably be best done
by the several Local Governments with the assistance of
their respective Heads of the Department of Education and,
when framed, they were to be subimtted to the Government
of India for approval. They were to be based entirely on
non-interference with the religious instruction conveyed in

the schools assisted. The grants were to be given so far as the requirements of districts and the funds at disposal permitted, to all schools which gave a good secular education and were under permanent local managements. No grants would be given to schools, except normal ones, which did not require from their pupils a fee for specific objects in preference to simple pecuniary grants for general expenses. The specific objects were stated to be, augmentation of salaries of head teachers, supply of junior teachers, foundation of scholarships, erection or repairing of school houses and provision of books. The amount and continuance of assistance would depend on the reports of the Government Inspectors. The effect of these grants should be, in no case, the substitution of public for private expenditure but the increase and improvement of education.

After making various observations which would guide the Local Governments in the framing of the rules for grants-in-aid, Dalhousie pointed out that they ought not be fettered by the necessity for referring every individual proposal for a grant-in-aid to the Supreme Government. It would be much better in every way that certain rules having been prepared by the Local Governments regarding grants-in-aid and having received the confirmation of the Governor-General-in-Council, the Local Governments should be left entirely free in the distribution of the grants. In like manner the aggregate annual amount of the grants having been fixed, the details of the expenditure should be left entirely to them.[69]

In January 1855 Dalhousie laid these proposals for working out the Despatch of 1854 before his Counil[70] and by February, he was able to report to Wood:

> The Education Scheme is, I think, now fairly launched, as far as the Supreme Government can do it, and the Subordinate Governments will work out the details quickly and with good will. The whole is being reported to you officially.[71]

Wood told him that he was very glad to hear this and thanked him very much 'for having taken so much interest in it'.[72] Indeed, Dalhousie took a keen interest in the working out of the Despatch. He hoped that if he lived, he would see 'the whole organized and in complete operation (so far as this can be affected at once)' before he left India.[73]

And he did not hope in vain. By the end of 1855 a distinct department for the superintendence of education was constituted. A Director-General of Public Instruction had been appointed by each Governor and Lt.-Governor, and in the Punjab; and suitable aid by inspectors and other means had been allocated to each of them. Provisional rules for regulating grants-in-aid had been sanctioned for the guidance of the Local Governments. And, finally a committee had been appointed for the purpose of framing a scheme for the establishment of universities at the Presidency towns of Calcutta, Madras and Bombay. By the time Dalhousie retired from India in March 1856 it was still engaged on that difficult task.[74]

Viewed as whole, it is cerainly not an exaggeration to say with Lee-Warner that 'in the matter of education, posterity has never given to Dalhousie the credit that is his due, not merely in organizing the departments of public instruction, but also in laying down the principles to be followed'.[75] It must be remembered that here Lee-Warner does not speak about Dalhousie's share in the making of the Despatch of 1854 as Professor Moor would have us believe[76] but refers to his achievement in working it out. Wood knew that to carry out such a scheme 'great labour must be imposed...and great difficulties must be encountered".[77] And while sending the Despatch, he had told Dalhousie :

I am aware that however good a scheme of this kind may be, the practical working of it is of more importance still and much more will depend upon the men appointed to carry the details out than on any skill in developing it.[78]

It is perhaps the irony of history that Wood's 'skill' which devised the Education Despatch of 1854 should be remembered and that the 'skill' which not only contributed to its development but put it into parctical shape in India should be forgotten.

REFERENCES

1. Despite the lapse of one hundred and twenty years since 1854 and the appointment of various Commissions, before and after 1947, the educational system in India remains basically unaltered.

2. 'The Composition of Wood's Education Despatch' *English Historical Review,* LXXX (1965), 85.

3. *Ibid.,* 76.

4. R.J. Moore, *Sir Charles Wood's Indian Policy* (Manchester, 1966), 108-9.

5. B.T. McCully, *English Education and the Origins of Indian Nationalism* (New York, 1940), 137.

6. *Ibid.,* 138.

7. Bourdillon to Wood. No date. *Wood Papers* (India Office Library), 12, para 34.

8. The letter is marked by these three words in pencil.

9. C.H. Philips, *The East India Company* (Manchester, 1940), 20-21.

10. Bourdillon to Wood, *Wood Papers,* 12, para 1.

11. *Ibid.,* para 2.

12. Bourdillon to Wood, *Wood Papers,* 12, para 11.

13. James Thomason was the Lt.-Governor of the North Western Provinces, 1848-53. For details about his administration, see D. Awasthi, *The Dawn of Modern Administration* (New Delhi, 1972).

14. *Ibid.,* para 17.

15. This impression is derived from the fact that the handwriting in the manuscript is different from Wood's.

16. *Wood Papers,* 12.

17. Written by Wood, *Wood Papers,* 12.

18. A West, *Recollections* (London, 1899), vol.1, 194. West served

under Wood when the latter became the first Lord of a Admiralty in Palmerstone's Government in February 1853 and was the author of a work on Wood's administration.

19. *Dalhousie Papers.* (Scottish Record Office), 207, fol.5.

20. *Ibid.,* fol.27

21. *Ibid.,* fols.27-28.

22. *Ibid.,* fol.28

23. M. Monier Williams, *Modern India and the Indians* (London, 1879), 297.

24. *Dalhousie Papers,* 207, fol. 25.

25. *Ibid.,* fols. 9-10.

26. *Dalhousie Papers,* 34/1.

27. Wood to Dalhousie, 24 July 1854. *Dalhousie Papers,* 57, fol.5.

28. *Dalhousie Papers,* 37/70

29. *Dalhousie Papers,* 39/18.

30. G.D. Bearce, *British Attitudes Towards India* (Oxford, 1961), 228-9.

31. See Chs. 2-4, PP. 22-141 in K Sen's 'Charles Wood and... the nineteenth century', (University of Sheffield MA Dissertation, 1960).

32. Dalhousie to Couper, 1854. J.G.A. Baird (ed.), *Private Letters of Marquess of Dalhousie* (Edinburgh, 1910), 324. Also see below.

33. 'The Composition of Wood's Education Despatch', English Historical Review, *op. cit., 77.*

34. See above.

35. See PP, 1852-53, XXXII, 1-639 for the Second Report from the Select Committee of the House of Lords on Education in India, comprising the Minutes of evidence and various written papers by noted educationists like Perry, Marshman, Trevelyan, Wilson, Cameron, etc.

36. McCully, *op. cit.,* 132-135.

37. Moore, *op. cit., 189.*

38. Wood to Dalhousie, 19 August 1853 *Dalhousie Papers,* 57, fol. 4.

39. Dalhousie to Wood, 4 October 1853. *Dalhousie Papers,* 62, fols. 5-6.

40. Dalhousie to Wood, 17 Novermber 1853. *Dalhousie Papers, 62,* fol. 1.

41. Dalhousie to Wood, 13 June 1854. *Dalhousie Papers,* 63, fol. 8.

42. Wood to Dalhousie, 24 July 1854. *Dalhousie Papers,* 57, fol. 5.

43. Dalhousie to Wood, 4 August 1854. *Dalhousie Papers,* 63, fols. 1-2.

44. Wood to Dalhousie , 9 August 1854. *Dalhousie Papers,* 57, fols. 2-3.

45. 'The Composition of Wood's Education Despatch' in *English Historical Review, op. cit.,*76.

46. *Ibid.,* 76-77.

47. P. Auber, *An Analysis of the Constitution of East India Company,* (London, 1826), 88-89.

48. Lord Broughton, *Recollections of a Long Life,* (London, 1911), vi, 195.

49. Wood to Marshman, 22 November 1853. *Wood Papers, India Board: Letter Book,* vol. 4. fol. 1.

50. Cf. 'He [Wood] was distinguished not by any originality of thought, but by a readiness to seek counsel wherever it might be found, by his judgement in evaluating opinions, and when he had set his course, by his effectiveness in disarming opposition and overriding objection', See Moore, *op. cit.* (note 4), 250.

51. Wood to Dalhousie, 24 July 1854. *Dalhousie Papers,* 57, fol. 4.

52. Wood to Colvile, October 1854, *Wood Papers, India Board: Letter Book,* vol.6, fol.119.

53. Dalhousie's Diary, 12 October 1854, quoted in M.N. Das, *Studies in Economic and Social Development of Modern India,* (Calcutta, 1959), 261.

54. Wood sent copies of the second draft of the Education Despatch to Macaulay, Prinsep, Perry and Marshman. See. *Wood Papers,* 12.

55. Dalhousie to Wood, 4 August 1854. *Dalhousie Papers,* 53, fol.2.

56. Dalhousie to Wood, 4 August 1854. *Ibid.,* fol. 2.

57. *Ibid.*

58. See Wood's speech on 8 August, Cole 1458-1463. Hansard's *Parliamentary Debates,* CXXXV.

59. Wood to Dalhousie, 9 August 1854. *Dalhousie Papers,* 57, fol. 3.

60. For a Comparative study of the attitudes of Wood and Dalhousie towards higher education, see M.N. Das, 'Bengal Past and Present'. *Journal of the Calcutta Historical Society*, LXXIV (1955), 151-8.

61. Wood to Dalhousie, 8 June 1854. *Dalhousie Papers*, 57, fol. 2. Wood expressed similar sentiments in many previous letters to Dalhousie and to Elphinstone. See Wood to Dalhousie, 24 April 1854 and 24 November 1853. Ibid., 3 and 5. Also Wood to Elphimstone, 24 January 1854, *Wood Papers, India Board: Letter Book*, vol.4, fols.104-6.

62. Court of Directors to the Governor-General, 19 July 1854, paras 1-10. See H. Sharp and J.A. Richey, *Selections from the Educational Records of the Government of India*, (Calcutta, 1922), ii, 364-7.

63. Dalhousie, *Diary*, 12 October 1854.

64. Monier Williams, *op. cit.*, 297.

65. *Dalhousie Papers*, 212, fols. 16-17.

66. Dalhousie to Wood, 7 Novermber 1854, *Dalhousie Papers*, 63.

67. *Ibid.*

68. *Dalhousie Papers*, 38/78.

69. *Ibid.*

70. Dalhousie to Wood, 21 January 1853. *Dalhousie Papers*, 64.

71. Dalhousie to Wood, 8 February 1853. *Ibid.*

72. Wood to Dalhousie, 26 March 1853. *Dalhousie Papers*, 58, fol.1.

73. Dalhousie to Wood, 8 February 1853. *Dalhousie Papers*, 64.

74. *Dalhousie Papers*, 212, fols. 16-17.

75. W. Lee-Warner, *The Life of the Marquis of Dalhousie*, (London, 1904), ii, 206.

76. The Composition of Wood's Education Despatch' in *English Historical Review*, *op. cit.*, 75.

77. Wood to Dalhousie, 23 December 1854. *Dalhousie Papers*, 57, fol. 2.

78. Wood to Dalhousie, 24 July 1854. *Ibid.*, fol. 5.

Chapter-IV

The Utilitarianism of Dalhousie and the Material Improvement of India*

In his final minute in March 1856, just on the eve of his departure from India, Lord Dalhousie, while reviewing the last eight years of his administration,[1] describes the railways, electric telegraph and uniform postage which he introduced into India as the "three great engines of social improvements".[2] The posterity certainly knows how correct Dalhousie's description was[3] but underlying this prophetic utterance of Dalhousie flows a subtle current of philosophy which few scholars working on the Dalhousie era have been able to detect and interpret. That philosophy was the philosophy of Jeremy Bentham and his faithful and able lieutenant, James Mill.[4] In his *History of British India* which Mill undertook before 1808 and published at London in three volumes in 1817,[5] Mill had questioned the values of the Indian society and suggested its reform on the Banthamite principles. The key to progress in India, Mill also pointed out, lay in the introduction of Western science and knowledge.[6] It is surprising that Dalhousie, though a staunch Tory, subscribed to this view and the natural alliance of the Benthamite administrator and the authouritative "Tory gentleman" which "was never fully achieved in England was achieved only in India".[7]

---

*   Appeared in *Modern Asian Studies,* Cambridge, February, 1978, Vol.12, Part-I, pp. 97-110.

Professor Eric Stokes in his classic work on *The English Utilitarains and India* has devoted only three pages to a discussion of the utilitarian character of Dalhousie's administration in India[8] but a broad analysis of the utilitarian influences which have shaped Dalhousie's policy towards the material improvement of India still remains to be made.

Born and brought up in an age which ideologically belonged to Bentham and his followers[9], it was indeed difficult for Dalhousie, though essentially a conservative, to escape their influence. Young states that "in discipleship or reaction no young mind of the thirties could escape their (the utilitarians'), influence. Bentham's alliance with James Mill, Mill's friendship with Malthus and Ricardo, had created a party, almost a sect, with formularies as compact as the Evangelical theology and conclusions not less inexorable".[10] Dalhousie gave first proof of his utilitarianism when in 1854 he joined Peel's cabinet which had succeeded Melbourne's[11] "as President of the Board of Trade[12]. While in Parliament, Macaulay, a friend of James Mill[13], who had fallen under the spell of utilitarian doctrines at Cambridege in 1818,[14] had advocated for state intervention in railways[15]; in Government Dalhousie laid before Peel "a sound and statesman like scheme" for placing British railways under the direct control of the state. Dalhousie's scheme was not accepted, for, in those days Parliament looked coldly upon any scheme which savoured of state interference with individual or class interests.[16]

But what Dalhousie could not achieve in England, he achieved in India and this achievement was not solely confined to railways but to other aspects of his programme for material improvement of India. This is because his governor-generalship respresented that type of authoritarian government which both Bentham and Mill had passed for as the best in India. Bentham thought that an absolute authority would be the best machine to produce the greatest happiness to the greatest number of people[17] and the British colonies like India appeared to the philosopher as the best fields for experimentation in reforms.[18] This explains why, despite his address to the National Convention of France in 1793 in an article "Emancipate your Colonies", he held diametrically opposite views about India and this he made clear by adding a postscript to an article on 24 June 1829[19], one year and a half after Bentinck had gone out to India as the Governor-General.[20] Similarly Mill who had gone so far as to maintain in his *History of British India* that no nation which did not have a representative legislature, chosen by universal suffrage, enjoyed security against oppression, thought that such institutions were not practicable in India[21]. It is true that Dalhousie was not the only Governor-General to wield absolute powers in India, his predecessors also did the same. But what is interesting to note here that unlike his predecessors Dalhousie actually looked upon himself as an Oriental monarch, the source of all power and dispenser of all favour. He could, therefore, easily write to the Lt. Governor of the North-Western Provices, a few months before his retirement from India : "By the end of April (1856), you know, I shall be 'O' er the hills and far awa'—and you will have to apply to a new Pharoah, for the sanctions you want".[22] He had a Council but it was essentially submissive—and in the event of necessity he could proceed to any part of India without it and could exercise all powers of the Governor-General-in-Council except those of legislation.[23] What was galling to him was the restrictions imposed on his powers by the Court of Directors at London. He could not view it with pleasure that for every measure he wanted to carry out in India he had to receive the sanction of the Court first and he made his complaint known privately as well as officially on more than one occasion.

How this absolute authority was to be exercised to destroy prejudices and bring about reforms in the society?

In other words, how the greatest-happiness principle was to be implemented by an absolute authority? Society consisted of an agglomeration of individuals, by nature existing in mutual isolation, and united solely by deliberate volitions. Some individuals were happy, some unhappy—which side outnumbered the other? This is the balance which one must strike whenever one would appreciate a law or a custom. And this simple operation of addition and substraction composed the entire intellectual task of an authoritarian reformer.[24] While in India, he acquainted himself "thoroughly with the system of government and its administration, with the condition, the resources and the wants of the country."[25] He made a clear distinction between those functions which must be carried out by an authoritarian government and those which were to be executed by a third party. While education, electric telegraph and the uniform postage came under the first category, railways under the second. The first group consisted of "works which affect the general well being of the community...and which producing no immediate return must be executed by the Government if they are to be formed at all".[26] Since the second group such as the introduction of railways would bring immense profits to some commercial groups in England, they must be executed by them.[27] There was another reason why he encouraged private enterprise in railways in India. In his own words "one of the greatest drawbacks to the advance of this country in material prosperity has been the total dependence upon the Government in which the community has placed itself, and its apparent utter helplessness to do anything for itself."[28] No doubt Dalhousie wanted to break this tradition by encouraging private enterprise in India. Though private enterprise was to be an improtant element in the introduction of railways, yet railways in India should be viewed as a national concern rather than as a private undertakings which was the case in England. He, therefore, urged strongly :

"I trust they [the East India Company] will ever

avoid the error of viewing Railways merely as private undertakings and will regard them as national works over which the Government may justly exercise, and is called upon to exercise, a stringent and statutory control. This control should not be an arbitrary right of interference, but a regulated authority, declared and defined by law—which is not to be needlessly or vexatiously exerted; but which in my humble judgement, is necessary at once for the interests of the state and for the protection of the public."[29]

Indeed, in any country the interests of the railway company and that of the community may be diametrically opposed to each other.[30] Dalhousie correctly visualised that the Government of India would be often called upon to protect the people from the encroachment of the railway company officers. In the the middle of 1855 people at Patna were greatly excited and agitated at the operations connected with the appropriation of land for railway purposes by the railway company officers.[31] At this the Government of India directed that no land should be appropriated by the Railway Commissioner until its owner was fairly compensated for its loss and that the railway company should be held responsible for any encroachment upon or injury to property in the preliminary survey for the railway and that every effort should be uniformly made to avoid injury to mosques, temples and places held in veneration by any class of community.[32] It was only just that the Government of India should exercise a supervisory control over the railway companies to prevent them from exploiting the public as well as from increasing their profit by raising railway fares at public expense. In the same year which witnessed the Patna incident, the railway returns were exhibiting a steady increase. The railway companies could not seize this opportunity to increase the railway fares as the *Friend of India* rightly commented:

"Fortunately, the Rail is under the absolute control of the Government and will therefore be regulated by that higher principle which belongs to the relation of sovereign and subject : not by the relation of the monopolist and his customers."[33]

In India, therefore, Dalhousie was able to translate his idea—certainly borrowed from the utilitarian doctrine—of bringing railways under the state control into reality.

As it has been stated earlier, a strong government was also necessary to destroy prejudices and bring about reform in the society, besides supervising works of public concern. For, the utilitarian idea of progress was not only an idea of a progress with the help of new scientific innovations such as railways and electric telegraph but also that of a progress with the reform of the existing social order. Bentham has earned an important place in the histroy of intellect by carrying the war of criticism and refutation, the conflict with falsehood and absurdity, into the field of practical evils.[34] Dalhousie approached the problems of infanticide, female education and the remarriage of the Hindu widows with the spirit of a Bentham. While criticising the existing postal system in India, the Benthamite influences on him were at their best :

"Years have passed since the inequality and injustice of such a system were recongnised and remedied in Great Britain by the Imperial Parilament...if it be unjust in England that the burden of postal charges, including those for the public correspondence of the state, should rest exclusively on one class, and if the injustice has been recognised in many states of Europe and America, the injustice is not lighter or less oppressive in India. If it were wise in England to remove every obstacle to free communication between man and man, to facilitate dissemination of knowledge and to correct with all prudent speed a sensible an admitted grievance, wisdom would dictate now the same liberality in legislation here.''[35]

In this connection the appointment of the Commissioners of Post Office by him to investigate into the abuses of the postal system is one of the most direct proofs of his utilitarianism he had offered during his stay in India. Indeed, the way in which he sought to execute his special measures for the material improvement of the people owes much to Bentham's ideas. In England the poor Law Commission, the Railway Board and other Central Agencies owed their origin to them. In India the origin of the departments of railways, electric telegraph and post office may be traced to the same influences which were at work in Dalhousie's mind. "My own opinion", he wrote on 30 June 1854, "has long been decidely in favour of placing a single authourity at the head of every public department. In that form only can sustain promptitude of action be maintained and real responsibility enforced."[36] He appointed a Consulting Engineer to head the department of railways, a Superintendent to head the department of electric telegraph and a Director-General to head the department of post office. They were supreme in all matters connected with their departments but were to act under the direct control of the Government of India. In the case of the department of post office, the Director-General had to surrender the power of appointing Post Master-Generals and other local officers but after their appointment they would be under his exclusive control. Dalhousie did not view this surrender of power on behalf of the Director-General with pleasure and till the end of his term he was trying to impress upon the Court the need for an absloute authourity on behalf of the Director-General which would, in turn, increase the entire control in the hands of the Government of India over the other local governments.

In the utilitarian philosophy of an authoritarian government, unity of authority is as essential as the uniformity of management. Dalhousie accepted this principle and he was always careful that his social measures should be uniform, in other words, systematic. He would extend the Thomason's system of vernacular education not only to the rest of the North Western Provices but also to the Bengal, Bihar and the Punjab. He was certainly glad to find that the Education Despatch of 1854 would provide a uniform system of eudcation for the whole of India. It was a "Vast Concern" and though its implementation would give a "Vast [amount] of trouble, it would produce...a commensurate Vast [amount] of good."[37] From the very beginning of the introduction of railways in India, he was careful that the railway gauges in India, unlike in England, should be unifrom:

> "The British legislature fell unconsciously and per-haps unavoidably into the mischievous error of permitting the introduction of two gauges [sic] into the United Kingdom. The numerous and grievous evils which arose from the permission are well-known, and will long be felt throughout all England. The Government of India has its power, and no doubt will carefully provide, that however widely the Railway system may be extended in this Empire in the time to come, these great evils shall be averted, and that uniformity of gauge [sic] shall be rigidly enforced from the first."[38]

He insisted that the railway codes in one Presidency should not vary from those in the other. Since the railways were an all-India enterprise, the codes to govern them should be uniform. Local government could modify them to suit local conditions but the basic codes must be the same for the three Presidencies.[39] Just as in the case of railways, so also in the case of the electric telegraph, he insisted that the rates of charges and the rules governing them should be same and uniform for all.[40]

It must not be thought that Dalhousie was able to translate his ideas into action without any hindrances. Almost

at every step particularly in the field of Western innovations—he had to encounter stiff opposition to his views
from the Court and the way he fought it and finally was
able to impose his arguments upon it was essentially that
of Bentham. In an article Mill thus describes Bentham's
method:

> "Bentham's method may be shortly described as
> the method of detail; of treating wholes by separat-
> ing them into their parts, abstractions by resolving
> them into things—classes and generalities by distin-
> guishing them into the individuals of which they are
> made up; and breaking every question into pieces
> before attempting to solve it."[41]

Dalhousie's method was also a method of detail. Just
as Bentham laying his subject before him for he day, thought
on, and set down his thoughts in page after page[42] so also
Dalhousie would "master a subject before" he decided on
it[43] and expressed his views in his minutes. He would divide
them into several sections. In the introductory sections he
broke up the subjets into several parts and dealt with each
of them in the following sections separately before coming
to a conclusion. While dealing with any controversial
question, he would first state the arguments of his opponents
(in most cases, the Court of Directors) and then refute them
one by one, and before concluding he would state his
argruments so forcibly as to succeed in imposing his own
views upon them on the question.[44] In his minute divisions,
he had, as Bentham had before him,[45] perpetual occasion
to compare, balance or contrast one proposition with another.
And like Bentham looking upon the language as the only
means through which this could be accomplished, he took
great care of it. Like that of Bentham, his style was also
simple, clear and powerful[46], "free of all qualification or
ornament" as Stokes says.[47] Arnold says that "the minutes
of Lord Dalhousie carefully edited, would add a valuable
tome to English classics, their rapid succession, their variety,

their pith and pointedness, can hardly be over praised; while their lucid statement of facts, with the complete mastery of details exhibited in them, are not more striking than the enlightened sentiments, the comprehensive policy, and the enlarged statemanship which pervade and animate many of them. Even on abstruse subjects, so quick was his mastery of technicalities, and so true his application of new principles that some of his improvised minutes are really exhaustive treatises."[48] His minutes on railways on 20 April 1853 was an important example of what Arnold has said. It ran to several hundred pages and was hailed by the contemporaries as "the text book for all future Railway projects in India."[49] If it had been the work only of a statesman, engineers would have been certain to assail it. If it had been the work simply of an engineer, statesman might have cast it aside.[50] But the minute was the work of an engineer—statesman—of a Governor-General who had mastered the "technicalities" of railways. In 1882 Hunter could comment that the minute "still faithfully" represented "the railway map of India...although modified in detail by Lord Mayo's reform of 1869."[51]

While "arguing all points with the preciseness of a Scottish logician."[52] John William Kaye points out, Dalhousie had displayed a lack of imagination in carrying out his measures for the material improvement of the people in India. "He could not understand", Kaye adds, "the tenacity of affection with which they clung to their old traditions."[53] But if Dalhousie lacked imagination, he did so because he was blinded to the Indian reactions, if any, by the extent of the benevolent impact his reforms and innovations would one day produce upon the people in India. As he said in connection with his programme for railways, "I...entertain a hope that in the years to come this great instrument of improvement may be extended over all the land, bringing with it the rich and numerous benefits it is calculated to produce."[54] In his final minute in 1856 he dwelt on the innumerable benefits his reforms and innovations would give to the people in India. On the other hand, there is evidence to show that he did not lack imagination and on more than one occasion he displayed his conservatism and admired Oriental culture. In Dalhousie Papers there are two special instructions from the Court of Directors to the Government of India regarding non-interference with the religion of the Indians. The instructions were dated 21 April 1847 and 19 January 1848 respectively.[55] Dalhousie must have studied them carefully and was able to say on 6 June 1854 :

> "During my administration I have carefully followed the traditional policy, which has been handed down to the Government of India, for its observance in all matters into which there enters a religious element."[56]

Despite the suggestions of the Council of Education to revolutionise the Hindu College and the Madrassa he felt it is to be "the duty of the Government to maintain in Calcutta, as heretofore, the Seminaries of that peculiar oriental learning which is cultivated by the great sects of Hindus and Musaulmans respectively."[55] He was equally anxious to preserve the old relics if they were worth preserving. When Gerorge Turnbull, the Railway Engineer, proposed to knock down the ruins of the old palace at Rajmahal, he did not agree. He believed that the East India Railway Company inherited the destructiveness of its race—that if there should be "any architectural rule [relic] within manageable distance of their line they invariably proposed to "knock it down", though everybody else was desirous of keeping it up."[58] He was happy that a railway viaduct across the Yamuna at Agra could be constructed on the Northern Line and not on the Southern Line close to Taj. As he observed," although a hearty friend to Railways and a steady advocate of the principle that everything should, so far as possible, be made to yield to the public convenience and advantage yet I do not think I could ever have brought myself to commit so hideous a sacrilege against all good taste, as to propose that a railway viaduct should be constructed within a few yards of Taj, and that the mean buildings of a railway station should be squatted under the walls of that matchless monument of human art.''[59]

It must, however, be remembered that Dalhousie never gave explicit expression to his beliefs in utilitarian principles. The classic example among some of Dalhousie's predecessors who had accepted utilitarianism as their second faith was provided by Bentinck. In a farewell dinner at Grote's house, just on the eve of his departure for India as its Governor-General, in December 1827, Bentinck had said to James Mill: ''I am going to British India but I shall not be Governor-General. It is you that will be Governor-General.''[60] Dalhousie never made such open declaration of his faith in utilitarianism. Again, unlike Elphinstone who was in close contact with Bentham through Strachey,[61] Dalhousie never came into contact with James Mill who had entered the East India House in 1819 after the publication of his voluminous *History of British India* in 1817[62] or with his son, John Stuart Mill who had joined his father in the East India House as a junior clerk in the Examiner's Office in 1823[63] and had firmly fixed utilitarian influence in India affairs,[64] Dalhousie's utilitarianism'', as Professor Stokes points out, ''was characteristic of his age. It was no longer a fixed programme derived from the texts of Bentham nor was it a set of intellectual dogmas. It was rather a practical cast of mind.''[65]

Yet there were occasions when he came very near to express his utilitarianism. His frequent references to his concerns about the interests of the community in India, like, ''the good of the communituy'', ''the interests of the public'', ''the welfare of the mankind', ''the largest aggregate amount of benefit for the people'', were so many acknowledgements of ''the Greatest Happiness Principle.''[66] In one of his letters to Couper, he states : "You will find me (I have a notion) a curious compound, of despot and radical. In truth I would be a despot for many radical changes, but not in the conventional sense of that "root and branch" designation."[67] "A despot for many radical changes", certainly means an authoritarian reformer as the utilitarians were and Dalhousie played that role in India successfully. In his farewell address to the inhabitants of Calcutta on 5 March 1856, he described himself as a servant of the state and spoke like a utilitarian philosopher:

"While we have a right to congratulate ourselves on what has already been done, while we may regard with complacency the introduction into the East of those great instruments of public benefit which Science has long since created in the West; while we may rejoice that measures have been already taken for opening new sources of public wealth, for ministering to the convenience of increasing the happiness, and for raising the mental and social condition of the endless millions, whom providence for its own wise ends has committed to our charge: I trust we still shall feel that all we have yet done must be regarded as no more than the first beginning of greater things that are to come."[68]

It is unfortunate that Dalhousie could not visualise the "greater things" that were "to come" in the wake of progress and improvement. These were seen by Elphinstone in the 1810's[69] Munro in the 1820's[70] Macaulay and Trevelyan[71] in the 1830's. All agreed that one day the material and moral progress of India would result in a demand for self government by the Indians. Macaulay had gone so far as to assert that if that day ever came, that would be the proudest achievement of the *British Raj* in India.[72] Dalhousie never contributed to the largehearted English liberalism of the time and tried to strengthen British grip over India by the introduction of railways and electric telegraph. His limitations if any were the limitations of the utilitarian doctrine of James Mill and Bentham who regarded India to be despotically governed for the happiness of the people. In this sense, Dalhousie was a true successor to Bentham and Mill. But before long it was James Mill's own son, John Struart Mill who in the third chapter of his *Considerations on Reperesentative Government* demolishes the fond theory entertained by many that the best government is "absolute power in the hands of an eminent individual"[73] and states categorically in his article on "Civilisation" that progress is followed by a demand among the people in the control of the government. In other words, it is as a result of material progress in any civilization "that power passes more and more from individuals, to masses: that the importance of the masses becomes constantly greater, that of individual less."[74]

No one will deny that Dalhousie's social policy contributed greatly to the material and moral improvement of India. From the Western point of view of civilisation, his administration was essentially an era of progress. "The Railway, the Electric Telegraph, the new and improved organization of large and important departments, these are but the more salient points of a domestic administration of which it is not too much to say, and History surely will say, that its almost every step has been either an improvement or a preparation for an improvement."[75] And histroy has surely said this. The real significance of his social policy is seen after his departure from India, not in the outbreak of the Mutiny, but in the decades which followed it. These years which were also years of progress[76] told their observers that greater things that were to come had come. In 1865 while concluding his works on Dalhousie, Arnold, a contemporary of Dalhousie, notices them and records : "We shall be expelled from India...We are making a people in India where hitherto there have been a hundred tribes but no people."[77] Another contemporary, the Duke of Argyll, also observes in the same vain: "When the records of our Emprie in the East are closed, Lord Dalhousie's administration will be counted with the greatest that have gone before it and that among the benefactors of the Indian people no name will have better place than his."[78] The uniform system of education, of railways, of telegraph and of uniform postage as well as the many social reforms which Dalhousie introduced into India were now producing their effects upon the Indian community. In 1867 Lord Salisbury could inform the House of Commons : "The impression produced on my mind whilst I was at the India Office was that I was watching a vast community, as it were, in the act of creation. The changes going on were so rapid; prejudices a thousand years old apperared to be so rapidly melting away : the agency in operation were so powerful; these great facilities of locomotion which have done so much for the rest of the world were having so strong an effect",[79]...Only eighteen years after Salisbury had said this the Indian National Congress came into existence[80] and at its first session at Bombay paid its tribute to Dalhousie: "The progress of Education throughout the different provinces of the Indian Empire is so great, and the facilities for intercommunication so various that we, who were hitherto strangers to each other as the Sikhs, the Mahratas, the Bengalees and Madrassis, consider ourselves as the people with the same grievances and with the same aspirations."[81]

Viewed as a whole, Dalhousie's *régime* contributed greatly to the transformation of Oriental India into Western India. The series of Western innovations he had introduced and the reforms he had carried out, Dalhousie thought, would strengthen the grip of the *British Raj* over India. It was perhaps the greatest limitation of Dalhousie that he failed to see the future that a modern country would give birth to a modern nation. In history things often happen which their authors do not intend them to happen and after they have happened they make them famous. In India today Dalhousie is remembered more as a catalyst in the growth of Indian nationalism than as a torch-bearer of British imperialism or as the man at the root of the Mutiny which swept the Indian sky in 1857.

REFERENCES

1. A reappraisal of Dalhousie's administration in India is long over due. In the absence of it, E. Arnold's *The Marquis of Dalhousie's Administration of British India,* in 2 vols. (London, 1862-5) and Sir W. Lee-Warner's *The Life of the Marquis of Dalhousie* in 2 vols. (London, 1904), still hold the field. M.N. Das's *Studies in the Econmic and Social Development of Modern India* (Calcutta, 1959) is informative but not illuminative.

2. *Parliamentary Papers,* (House of Commons), 1856 Vol.45, 245, p. 16, para 24.

3. The finest tribute has been paid by, Jawaharlal Nehru, the first Prime Minister of Independent India in his Preface to L.K. Shridharani, *Story of the Indian Telegraphs.* (New Delhi, 1953) : "A person living two thousand years ago would have recognised the main features of human existence [in India] right up to the middle almost of the 19th century...Then came the great change heralded by the railway and the telegraph which has progressively altered the very texture of human life."

4. See Élie Halévy, *La Formation du Radicalisme Philosophique,* in 3 vols. (Paris, 1901-4), vol.2, p. 286.

5. The British Museum possesses a copy of this publication of 1817. Professor Eric Stokes incorrectly states in his preface to *The English Utilitarians and India,* (Oxford, 1959) that Mill undertook this work in 1808 and finished it in 1819.

6. See Books II and III in James Mill, *History of British India,* in 3 vols. (London, 1817), vol.1, pp. 91-648. Also Halévy. *op.cit.,* p.268. Halévy regards Mill's *History of British India* as "un instrument de propaganda Benthamique".

7. G.M. Young, *Victorian England* (London, 1936), p. 54

8. Eric Stokes, *op.cit.,* pp.248-51.

9. J.M. Kaye and G.B. Malleson, *History of the Indian Mutiny of 1857-8,* in 6 vols. (London, 1888-9), vol.1, pp. 259-60.

10. Yong, *op.cit.,* p.8.

11. L.J. Trotter, *Life of the Marquis of Dalhousie* (London, 1889), pp. 12-13.

12. A study of Dalhousie's *Papers* as President of the Board of

Trade in England provides a background understanding to Dalhousie's Governor-Generalship of India, 1848-56. The total number of those *Papers* which have been scientifically processed by the archival staff at the Scottish Record Office, Edinburgh, is 76.

13. A. Bain, *James Mill* (London, 1882), p. 370.

14. Eric Stokes, *op.cit.,* p. XIV.

15. Macaulay's speech has been quoted in Young, *op.cit.,* p.53.

16. Trotter, *op.cit.,* pp. 19-20.

17. Bentham to Malcolm, 2 June 1824, Portfolio No.10, Folder No.22, p.158 in *Bentham Papers.* In the Collection of *Bentham Papers* at the University College Library, London, Boxes X and CLXIX show Bentham's great interest in Indian affairs.

18. Halevy, *op.cit.,* Vol. 3, pp. 379-380.

19. J. Bowring (ed.), *Works of Jeremy Bentham* in 11 vols. (London, 1843), Vol.4, p. 418.

20. As yet there has not been any comprehensive account of Bentinck's Governor-Generalship of India, but, for his life, see D. Boulger, *Lord William Bentinck,* (Oxford, 1892).

21. A Bain, *op.cit.* p. 369.

22. Dalhousie to Colvin, 20 December 1855. *Dalhousie Papers* 117. Letter No.151.

23. Lee-Warner, *op.cit.,* Vols. 2, p. 227.

24. Élie Halévy, *Histoire du peuple Anglais au XIXe Siecle* in 5 vols. (Paris, 1912-32), vol.1, p. 551.

25. *Dalhousie's Diary,* Part 1, 1848, quoted in M.N. Das, *op.cit.,* p.45.

26. *Dalhousie Papers* 31/111.

27. *Ibid.*

28. *Ibid.*

29. *Dalhousie Papers* 22/116.

30. Lt. Col. a. Cotton, *Public Works in India.* (London, 1859), p. 81.

31. Court to Dalhousie, 26 September 1855. *Railway Despatches to Bengal and India,* vol. 2, pp. 183-5.

32. *Ibid.*

33. *Friend of India,* Serampore 17 May 1855.

34. John Stuart Mill, "Bentham" in *Dissertation and Discussions* in 2 Vols. (London, 1859), p.337.

35. *Dalhousie Papers* 27/367.

36. Qouted in Lee-Warner, *op.cit.,* Vol. 2, p. 189.

37. Dalhousie to Halliday, 29 August 1854. *Dalhousie Papers* 117. Letter No.50.

38. *Dalhousie Papers* 22/116

39. *Dalhousie Papers* 38/25.

40. *Dalhousie Papers* 36/39.

41. J.S.Mill, *op.cit.*, pp. 339-340.
42. Bowring, *op,cit.*, vol.I, p. ii.
43. Dalhousie to Wood, 29 June 1854. *Dalhousie Papers* 63.
44. This impression is formed by a study of several hundred minutes of Dalhousie consisting of 26 volumes at the Scottish Record office, Edinburgh.
45. Bowring, *op.cit.*, Vol. I, p.8.
46. *Ibid., p. 6.*
47. Stokes, *op.cit.*, p. 249.
48. Arnold, *op.cit.*, Vol. 2, pp. 322-3.
49. *Friend of India.*, Serampore, 8 September 1853.
50. *Ibid.* 22 September 1853.
51. W.W. Hunter, *The Indian Empire* (London, 1882), *P. 432.*
52. J.W. Kaye and G.B. Malleson, *op.cit.*, Vol.I, p. 261.
53. *Ibid.*, p. 261.
54. *Dalhousie Papers 22/116.*
55. *Dalhousie Papers 131.*
56. *Dalhousie Papers 37/70.*
57. *Dalhousie Papers 34/1.*
58. *Dalhousie Papers 38/34.*
59. *Dalhousie Papers 41/10.*
60. Bentham to Young, 28 December 1827. Bowring, *op.cit,* Vol. 10, pp. 516-7. Bentham reproduced it as he later heard from Mill in his letter to Young.
61. Kenneth Ballhatchet, *Social Policy and Social Change in Western India,* (London, 1957), pp. 34-6.
62. Eric Stokes, *op.cit.*, p. xii.
63. A Bain, *John Stuart Mill,* (London, 1882) p. 32.
64. Eirc Stokes, *op.cit.* p. xii.
65. *Ibid.*, p. 249.
66. Bowring, *op.cit.*, Vol. I. p. 20.
67. Dalhousie to Couper, 23 March 1856. J.G.A. Baird (ed.), *Private Letters of the Marquess of Dalhousie* (Edinburgh, 1910), p. 372.
68. *Dalhousie Papers* 218.
69. Elphinstone quoted in P. Griffth *Modern India,* (London, 1957), p. 62.
70. Munro quoted in Ramsay Muir, *The Making of British India,* (Manchester, 1915), pp. 284-5.
71. C.E. Trevelyen, *on the Education of the People of India,* (London, 1838), pp. 192-5.
72. Macaulay's speech of 10 July 1833 in the House of Commons See Hansard, *Parliamentary Debates,* vol. 19, col. 536.
73. See Chapter III, pp. 45-69 in John Mill's *Considerations on Representative Government.*

74. John Stuart Mill, "Civilization" in his *Dissertations and Discussions,* p. 163. Because of the influence of his father's *History of India* on him, he, however, denied "the applicability of his theories of liberty and representative government to the conditions prevalent in Eastern dependencies. See R. Iyer, "Utilitarianism and All That" in *St. Antony's Papers* No.8 South Asian Affairs, I, p. 14."

75. Farewell address by the Lt. Governor of Bengal to Dalhousie on 13 February 1856 *Dalhousie Papers,* 218, pp. 7-8.

76. T. Prichard, *The Administration of India.* in 2 vols. (London, 1869), covering the period from 1859-1868.

77. E. Arnold, *op.cit.,* vol.2 p. 388.

78. The Duke of Argyll, *India under Dalhousie and Canning* (London, 1865), p. 68.

79. Speech of Lord Salisbury (Viscount Cranborne) on 24 May 1867. See Hansard, *Parliamentary Debates.* Vol. 187, col. 1075.

80. Briton Martin's *New India, 1885* (Bombay, 1969-70) should be read with Anil Seal's *The Emergence of Indian Nationalism* (Cambridge, 1968) and S.R. Mehrotra's *The Emergence of the Indian National Congress* (Delhi, 1971) which provide a background understanding to the birth of the Indian National Congress.

81. Proceedings of the 3rd Day, 30 December 1885; in *Proceedings of the First Indian National Congress* at Bombay, 28-30 December 1885, p. 90.

Chapter-V

THE GENESIS OF CURZON'S UNIVERSITY REFORM, 1899-1905*

In 1904, Lord George Curzon, Viceroy of Government in India, was the initiator and moving force of the enactment of the Indian Universities Act. This law intended to introduce radical changes into the five existing universities at Calcutta, Bombay, Madras, Lahore and Allahabad. Among these were an enlargement of the functions of the university; reduction in the size of the university senates; introduction of the principles of election; statutory recognition of the syndicates where university teachers were to be given an adequate representation; stricter conditions for the affiliation of colleges to a university; definition of the territorial limits of the universities, provision for a grant of Rs. 5 lakh a year for five years for implementing these changes to the five Indian universities and finally powers to the government to make additions and alterations while approving the regulations passed by the senates.[1] The Act, which had not found favour with the educated Indians, faced problems when the government set about to carry it out. No sooner had the provisional syndicates been chosen than the validity of the directions issued by the Chancellor of the Bombay University who had ordered that the election should be held by the faculties, was challenged in the Bombay High Court;[2] it was soon clear that similar action was going to be taken

---

* Appeared in *Minerva,* London, December, 1988, Vol. XXVI, No.4, pp. 463-492.

at Calcutta also and that the controversy would soon "extend to Madras, Allahabad, and Lahore and that litigation may become general".[3] Curzon wanted to put a speedy end to the doubts raised about the interpretation of the Indian Universities Act and about the validity of some of the directions issued under it by the Chancellors by legislation as suggested by the Governor of Bombay,[4] and introduce a bill in his Legislative Council validating the action of the Chancellors and the constitution of the senates and the syndicates.[5] The validating bill was passed into law on 10 February 1905. It provided that all directives purporting to have been constituted under the Indian Universities Act of 1904 had been duly issued and constituted.[6]

Curzon became preoccupied with the question of university reform from the very beginning of his term as the Viceroy of India in the last week of December 1898 and passed the Indian Universities Act towards the end of his term in 1904-05. However, his universities reform has not till now received the attention that it deserves from scholars working on Curzon or Curzonian era in India. Based entirely on *Curzon and Hamilton Papers*, Government of India records and reports as well as other contemporary sources including newspapers and proceedings of the Indian National Congress, this paper attempts to delineate the state of higher education in India before Curzon, Curzon's strategy to bring it under government control and an analysis of the factors other than academic which persuaded. Curzon to take this plunge.

II

On the eve of the enactment of the Indian Universities Act of 1904, while addressing the convocation of the University of Calcutta, Curzon observed that he "now" occupied the unusual position of the last chancellor of an old regime, addressing the last senate and the last syndicate of an era that was about to disappear. "There may be some'', he continued, ''who think that they see in the Vice-Chancellor and myself the two chief executioners, about to admonish their victims before leading them to the scaffold, and who may think that the position is one of some pain-fulness and restraint. But I can assure this convocation on behalf of my honourable colleagues as well as for myself that we entertain no such feelings. For the patient in our view is in no wise doomed to extinction, but is about to reappear with a fresh lease of life; and the instruments of the sentence held in their hand, not the executioner's axe, but the phial that contain the elixir of a new and happy resurrection.''[7]

As per Curzon's declaration at the convocation, the object of the Indian Universities Act was to cure the Indian universities of the various ills since associated with their birth. And the majority of the ills which had plagued uni-versities could be traced to the Acts of Incorporation passed by the Governor-General and Viceroy, Lord Canning in January 1857, which provided for their establishment at Calcutta, Bombay and Madras. The direction to set up these universities on the model of the University of London was provided by the Education Despatch of 1854 which was received by Canning's predecessor, Lord Dalhousie. And Dalhousie himself would have taken up immediate steps to establish them but for an ambiguity in the wording of the paragraph relating to their establishment which asked him to report to London about the precedures to be adopted.[8] Accordingly Dalhousie set up a committee and it was on the recommendations of this committee that the Acts of Incorporation were passed.

The preambles in the Acts of Incorporations estab-lishing the three universities were identical - they defined the objects of the universities to be the ''ascertaining by means of examination the persons who have acquired pro-ficiency in different branches of Literature, Science and Art and of rewarding them by Academic Degress as evidence of their respective attainments.'' There was to be a chancellor, a vice-chancellor and fellows, both ex-officio and ordinary who together would constitute the ''Body Politic and Corporate'' for each of the three universities. The number of the fellows excluding the chancellor and vice-chancellor was to be less than thirty. While the ex-officio fellows were to hold the fellowship during their official tenure only, the ordinary fellows were to be appointed by government for life—vacancies in their ranks were caused only by death, resignation or permanent retirement from India in the case of European officials or by cancellation of appointment by goverment.[9]

In 1882 the Punjab University was established by a special Act of Incorporation and in 1887, another special Act of Incorporation established the fifth Indian university at Allahabad. The general framework of these two special Acts of Incorporation was similar to the Acts of 1857 though power was given to the senates of Punjab and the Allahabad universities ''to appoint or provide for the appointment of Professors and Lecturers''[10]—a privilege which was denied by the Acts of Incorporation to the first three universities at Calcutta, Bombay and Madras in 1857. The first three universities were deliberately intended to be the examining universities only, in the same sense and on the same model as the then University of London, thereby ignoring an important advice of the Education Despatch of 1854 which suggested possible institution of ''professorships for the purpose of the delivery of lectures in various branches of learning for the acquistion of which, at any rate in an advanced degree, facilities do not now exist in other institutions in India''.[11] When Lahore and Allahabad got this privilege in 1882 and 1887 respectively, the Indians had asked for its extension to Calcutta, Bombay and Madras but European officials closely connected with the university had contested it on two grounds: first that the demand for constitutional expansion was fictitious in as much as the place of a teaching university had in reality been taken by the collegiate system which had sprung into existence since 1857 and second that it would be vain and foolish to constitute professorships or lecturerships for higher students than those who attended the college lectures because of the absence of such students, courses and any funds forthcoming for the endowment.[12] In the case of the Punjab University only, the endowment came in the form of a grant of Rs. 12000 a year from the Government of India for maintaining the Oriental institutions and the classes in Oriental learning.[13]

However, the most glaring defect of the Acts of Incorporation was in the appointment of the fellows to the senates of these universities. These fellows were appointed for life and not for a special period and there was no upper limit to the number of the fellows to be appointed though the minimum was fixed at 30.[14] At Allahabad the minimum was as much number [15] but at Lahore it was raised to 50.[16] The number of fellows steadily rose at Calcutta from 40 in 1857 to a maximum of 220 in 1890. Lord Lansdowne, in his Convocation Address on 18 January 1890, recognised the anomaly and proposed gradually to bring about its reduction but how small an advance had been made in this direction could be seen from the fact that when Curzon came to India in the last week of December 1898, the number still stood at 200 and he helped by "natural causes" and by his refusal to exercise the right of nomination, had been able to bring it to a little over 180 in 1901.[17] As regards the composition and qualifications of the 180 fellows exclusive of those who had been returned by election, the practice had been for the chancellor to invite recommendations from the Lieutenant Governor of Bengal, as representing the local government, from the vice-chancellor, as familiar with the working of the senate and from such representative persons he might care to consult. The result had been that the fellowship had come to be regarded as a sort of titular reward, conferred without much reference to the academic qualifications of the recipient, but rather as a stage of promotion in an Indian career. Prominent English officials and prominent Indians had been thus honoured though the former as a rule recognised no answering obligations. A good many drifted away from Calcutta into other provinces and posts although their names continued to block the list. Of those who continued in Bengal, a large number never attended. The list actually included the name of the Lieutenant Governor of the North-Western Provinces, although he was chancellor of his own university at Allahabad, and that of the Lieutenant Governor of the Punjab, though he was similarly chancellor of his university at Lahore. From time to time names had been recommended by the local goverment and accepted by the chancellor, for the special object of giving due recognition of special interests such as medicine and engineering. The result had been that the list of the nominated fellows was on the whole a distinguished list but as Curzon later pointed out "it is largely an absentee list: and the distinction that it reflects is official or professional rather than academic."[18]

In 1891, the privilege of election on a limited scale was conceded by Lord Lansdowne to the graduate of the university on an experimental basis and there was no pledge of its continuance. The qualifications laid down both for the electoral body and the elected were M.A.s. (B.A.s. before 1867) and holders of higher degrees in any faculty—in other words the electorate could choose only from among themselves.[19] This restriction was imposed on a reluctant senate to prevent election of political agitators from out-side. However, the slack and precipitate standard of quali-fication formulated in 1891 had resulted in the creation of a large and heterogeneous electorate scattered throughout Burma, Assam, Bengal, the Central Provinces and Ceylon, a cleverly organized system of canvassing, and a thoroughly undistinguished list of nominees. Of the 24 fellows elected since 1891, two had died. Of these, four had been chosen on specific grounds in exercise of a power by government in 1892 to reserve occasional vacancies for the Faculties of Medicine and Engineering or for eminence in education and literature. Of the remainder, 16 are practising lawyers and none of them was qualified for election by his degree in the Faculty of Law, that is, none was a D.L. They were all nominally elected by reason of their attainments in the Faculty of Arts, but only three of their number had obtained a first class in Arts, several only a second and some even a third. The whole of the lawyers came from unaided colleges where there had been no government supervision. Of the whole 22, only 2 or 3 were engaged in bonafide educational work and these were only elected in the reserved categories. Secondly, election was only secured by systematic and elaborate canvassing. Lists were kept by "the Vakils of the Elections" who having taken their degrees, had dispersed throughout India. Agents were employed to hunt them out and canvass them; and very considerable expense was incurred. No candidate had a chance of being returned who did not resort to these methods and was not supported by "the Vakils' Party". The system whether looked at from the point of view of methods or of men seemed to stand equally condemned. It was felt that any chancellor who "acquiesees in its continuance is shutting his eyes while a weapon is being forged which will ultimately extrude European standards and influence from the Senate altogether, and will hand over its government to a clique of political *frondeurs* who have no interest in Education."[20]

The syndicate of the Calcutta University which was the real governing body of the senate which was the nominal and statutory governing body of the university was in the anomalous position of having no statutory origin. No mention was made of it in the Act 1857 but its origin could be traced to an interpretation of clause VIII of the Act of

Incorporation which gave the chancellor, vice-chancellor and fellows powers to control university affairs as well as to make and alter any bye-laws and regulations in general, touching all matters whatever regarding the university.[21] The senate had not only almost completely abdicated its functions to the syndicate but its own annual meeting for purposes of bussiness was held at the most inconvenient season of the year : on the third Saturday in April, when the majority of the Europeans were absent from calcutta, as Maclean, the Vice Chancellor of the Calcutta University later reported to Curzon.[22]

The universities, thus set up by the Acts of Incorporation in 1857 were affiliating universities and no geographical limits to the areas of affiliation were indicated. The Calcutta University, for example, functioned not merely for Bengal, but for Burma, Assam, the Central Porvinces, and Ceylon and the affiliated institutions spread over from Simla and Mussorie to Indore and Jaipur, and from Jaffna and Batticaloa to Sylhet and Chittagong. Managed by their own governing bodies, the affiliated colleges were not part of the university—not all of them were residential institutions with a history or tradition, created mostly through the generosity of some philanthropic societies, missionary bodies, wealthy Indians, interested in spreading the light of enlightenment, but for most part collections of lecture rooms, and class rooms, and laboratories. They had no control over the courses of study which were prescribed by the university and their only function seemed to be to prepare students for the examinations which were again conducted by the university. Since a large number of colleges—government, aided and unaided—were affiliated with each of the three universities, it follows the rules for affiliation framed by the university were not very strict and indeed the first affiliation rules prepared by the Calcutta University in February 1857, for example only demanded from the college seeking affiliation with it a declaration, countersigned by at least two members of the Senate, of the staff and courses of study for the previous two years and of the institution's ability of imparting education up to the standard of B.A. degree.[23] Despite the Hunter Commission's attempt in 1882 to follow a stricter application of rules relating to affiliation, the growth in the number of affiliated colleges continued unabated so that by the time Curzon came to India, the total number of affiliated colleges in the whole of British India was 191, of which 145 were Arts Colleges and the rest Professional Colleges including Law (30), Teaching (5), Agriculture (3), Medicine (4) and Engineering (4). [24]

It would seem that these universities were then not merely examination bodies as their influences were extended far beyond examination by their practical power to refuse or admit the affiliation of colleges. They were independent of the education departments set up in the provinces of British India as per the direction of the Education Despatch of 1854. While an education department could exercise control over the government and aided colleges, it had no control over the private colleges which had "the chief part in the education of undergraduates" of the universities. The education departments were unable to banish politics from the unaided colleges where the managers and professors were likely to educate their pupils "in all the political and financial fallacies" antagonistic to the British connection. The number of such unaided colleges imparting legal education was particularly high in Bengal where the law students perhaps more than any other class of students were prone to politics and it was feared that the government had made a mistake "to let the control of legal education go entirely out of its hands" by not providing a properly instituted Government Law College in Calcutta as in Madras and Bombay.[25]

It is obvious that the affiliated colleges in different parts of British India could not be expected to maintain a uniform and high academic standard as there had not been a separate education department in the Government of India as in England with an organisation and a staff of its own to supervise higher education in the whole of British India. As a matter of fact, Madras normally turned out considerably more graduates than Calcutta and many more than Bombay, Allahabad and Punjab put together arousing doubts about the standard at Madras and many of the new affiliated colleges that came into existence as a result of the local and private effort before Curzon came, were "week, understaffed and incapable of affording the individual attention either to the needs of the student or of providing the varied courses of study, practical as well as literary",[27] so reported the Calcutta University Commission almost more than a decade and a half later in 1917.

III

Within three months of his coming to India as the Governor-General and Viceroy of India, Curzon's confrontation with the Calcutta University began in March 1899 when he came to know that the university had frustrated the Bengal Government's attempt to introduce William Lee-Warner's *Citizen of India* as a text book. As per the clause of the Acts of Incorporation establishing universities in India, the senates alone enjoyed the power of prescribing text books in affiliated colleges and since they were independent of government control, they enjoyed it and often took delight in slighting and thwarting the proposals put forward to them by the local governments. The Under Secretary of State, Arthur Godley, was a friend of Lee-Warner[28] and Curzon was both amazed and disgusted to find that Lee-Warner's "excellent manual" could not be introduced into any government schools and colleges in India because the Text Book Committee on which there was a majority of "Babus and only one government representative, had declined to admit it."[29] He informed

Hamilton, the Secretary of State, that he was going upto Simla to think over how "the management of our education system" could be brought under "central authority and government control"[30] "I have seen enough to know", Curzon wrote to Godley, "that in its desire to decentralise, government has surrendered its control to a very dangerous degree, and that the Local Governments, inspired by their attractive example, have also forefeited a good deal of their necessary authority. In fact the management of Education has gradually drifted into the hands of Committees or bodies upon which Englishmen are often in a numerical minority, who exercise their power in mischievous independence of Government."[31] It was because of this Burke's *French Revolution* which was "certainly dangerous food for Indian students" could be selected as a text book.[31a]

While at Simla, Curzon gave much thought to the subject of education. Godley told him that if Woodburn's observation that the Calcutta University "alone in India, is independent of the Local Government and its delight is to slight and thwart it" were correct, "it would seem to be in need of your reforming hand."[32] However, more information was needed before the idea of reform could be mooted. Curzon consulted Sir Staffordd Northcote and Lord Northbrook both of whom were then in England besides consulting Woodbrun. The consultation of Northbrook was particularly useful because he, as Charles Wood's Secretary drafted that celebrated Education Despatch of 1854[33] which provided for the setting up of the first three universities of Calcutta, Bombay and Madras. He also asked his secretary, Luson as well as Fraser, a member of his Council, to make elaborate comments on Cotton's *Quinquennial Review of the Progress of Education from 1892-3 to 1896-7* and when they were ready, he made some observation on their comments which provided the basis for the issue on 28 October 1899 the Resolution of the Government of India on Education identifying the areas where government control was necessary.[34] However, he did not follow it up by other administrative acts and orders since he did not consider the moment opportune for it. Heavily occupied with the famine and the frontier problems, he had no other alternative but to move slowly in the field of education. As a matter of fact, he had been a firm believer in the familiar axiom about going slow. He knew that "the prudent" general reconnoitred his country before he delivered the final assault.[35] It was time now for surveying the field of university education in India as far as Curzon was concerned.

And so, much of his time was taken up by his thorough and absorbing investigation into the subject of higher education since 1857 as well as in selecting a successor to Maclean whose term as the Vice-Chancellor of the Calcutta University was coming to an end. Curzon's immediate choice was one of his personal friends, the Bishop of Calcutta, who "would assist me in the schemes which I have in view for co-ordinating and controlling the higher education of this country."[36] However, Woodburn pointed out that one reason at least why the office was so frequently given to the high court that the pleaders who preponderated in the senate, were amenable to no one else but a judge.[37] Woodburn anticipated "stormy times" in the senate during the next two years in view of Curzon's scheme of controlling higher education and there would, therefore, be some advantage in having as influential a president of the senate as could be found for the period.[38] "And the only person I can think of as an alternative to the Bishop", he wrote, "is Mr. Raleigh" who was then a member of Curzon's Legislative Council since there was at the moment no judge available on the bench who would fit the post.[39] Curzon agreed[40] and towards the end of August 1900, he appointed Raleigh as the Vice-Chancellor of the Calcutta University. Raleigh like Curzon, was an undergraduate and a graduate of Balliol College, Oxford, under Professor Jowett and later became a Fellow of All Souls under Sir William Anson. While Curzon had been "swept of his feet in the mill-race of English politics", Raleigh became an Oxford Don[41] and Curzon hoped that Raleigh's abilities and academic knowledge would now find fuller scope in this new assignment.[42] Aided by Raleigh who "had the leisure, as well as the inclination to devote himself more exclusively to university affairs"[43] Curzon prepared to address himself to "the most difficult perhaps and certainly most delicate" of all his tasks, as Dawkins wrote to him.[44] Untill the rains came at Simla, Curzon suffered from "a good deal more of personal weakness and back pain than last year" but since the rains came he felt much better and was able to devote his full attention to his scheme.[45]

By 23 February 1901 his scheme was ready, when he recorded an extremely long minute on the subject, revealing his tremendous capabilities for hard work, for which he had a great reputation at Oxford, and for which he almost impaired his health in India just as Dalhousie had actually done before him.[46] The main thrust of his arguments in the minute was that legislation was necessary to (a) enlarge the functions of the Indian universities from examination to teaching, (b) regulate the number, tenure and qualifications of the fellows as well as to maintain a proper balance between Europeans and Indians, officials and non-officials, and between the various faculties or professions, (c) reconstitute the electorate by adding residential qualifications among the graduates just as the Convocation of Oxford now consisted of resident M.A.s. or rather such graduates as were capable of coming to the senates to vote as well as by laying down some academic or educational standard which was necessary for election to a fellowship at Oxford, as a qualification for election here, (d) provide a statutory status to the syndicate which was the real executive body of the university, (e) narrow the geographical limits/areas of each university, (f) strengthen the law relating to the recognition and affiliation of colleges as well as withdrawal of recognition or affiliation in cases in which discipline had been relaxed and the standard too much lowered, (g) curtail power of the boards of studies which prescribed text books for the colleges as well as regulate the courses of instruction of the candidates reading for the university examination and finally there was the question of revocation of the university degrees in cases where the holder had been convicted by a criminal court.[47] After listing the areas for legislation to tighten control over universities, Curzon felt that his plate was not full:

> "There are doubtless other subjects affecting the case for or against legislation which have not occurred to me, or of which I am ignorant...There also remains the question as to the competence of the Government of India to reform (either by legislative or by executives action) the University of Calcutta without reference to the case of the universities of Madras and Bombay; and even if the competence be indisputable, the experience or desirability of the same."[48]

It is, therefore, necessary to consult a body of expert opinions and six months after he had drafted the proposals for the university reform, he summoned a conference at Simla to look for the light at the end of the tunnel.

The first educational conference in India which met at Simla on 2 September 1901 was attended by, besides Curzon and members of his Council, the vice-chancellors of the universities of Calcutta, Bombay and Madras, the directors of public instruction in Bengal, Bombay, and Madras, the North-Western Provinces and the Punjab, Inspector-General of Education in the Central Provinces, Principal of the Deccan College at Poona, Principal of the School of Arts in Madras, Reporter on Economic Products to the Government of India and finally Curzon's Secretary Risley.[50] No Indian expert was invited though the conference was going to discuss "confidentially"[51] upon a subject which concerned the Indians most. ''The private...hole and corner character of the Conference'' became a subject matter of much discussion among the Indians and so Curzon thought of opening the conference with a statement which could be communicated to the press. In it he would outline the whole of the points upon which ''our system'' from the top to the bottom seemed to be deficient and should indicate the line upon which, tentatively at any rate, the reform ought to proceed. ''India is a country'', Curzon wrote to Hamilton,

> ''Where you can do almost everything provided that you allow your critics and opponents to have their say. I shall, therefore, invite the fullest discussion on all the points to be mentioned by me...I think it very likely that in the case of universities for the reform of which we shall almost inevitably be compelled to resort to legislation, I shall have to appoint a small preliminary commission to go round and take evidence at Calcutta, Madras, and Bombay and allow the instructed M.A.s. and B.A.s. who swarm at these capitals to have their say in advance.''[53]

Curzon himself meticulously planned and drafted the *strictly confidential* agenda papers. The first subject to be taken up for discussion by the conference was obviously university education. In his *strictly confidential* agenda papers, he had listed thirteen items on the subject. They included among others, scope and character of Indian universities, government of Indian universities, question of academic standards, affiliation of colleges and recognition of schools, selection of text books and courses of instruction and finally, ''is a commission desirable?''[54] Curzon divided the item on the government of Indian universities into three parts. The first part related to the question of the reform of the senates, the second to that of the election of the fellows and the third to that of the composition and function of the syndicates.[55]

As the discussions on university education advanced, it became more and more apparent to the members who took part in them that there had been "a total lack of system, an ignorance of principles, and a want of uniformity in practice, that have reduced education in India to a state almost of chaos."[56] On 10 september the deliberations over university education were over, the delegates having passed unanimously no fewer than 45 "strictly confidential" resolutions, [57] each one of them drafted by Curzon himself.[58] The delegates emphatically declared in favour of a thorough constitutional reform of the universities in India. They also recommended that the powers of government in respect of affiliation, recognition and text-books should be strengthened; that a Director-General of Indian education should be appointed; that the rules for examination and degrees should be co-ordinated and improved, and that the institution of hostels should be encouraged and that a minimum rate of fees should be fixed.[59] The conference was also in favour of the decision of Curzon to appoint a commission to examine the question of university education in all its aspects.

In a telegram to Hamilton on 13 January 1902 Curzon proposed to appoint six persons as permanent members of the commission including Raleigh who was to be the Chairman.[61] The other five were Hewett, Pedler, Bourne, Mackichan and Syed H. Bilgrami.[62] Bilgrami was the only Indian representative and when the appointment of the commission was made public after obtaining Hamilton's approval, the absence of a Hindu among the six permanent commissioners created a great stir since the Hindus had "the largest interest in the educational problems that were to be considered." Surendra Nath Banerjee a dismissed member of the Indian Civil Service on filmsy grounds, who had earlier led the Civil Service Agitation in 1876-7 raised "a vigorous protest" in the columns of the *Bengalee* which he himself edited against "this ostracism of the Hindu element."[63]

The Indian public opinion supported Banerjee's view and Curzon had no other alternative but to send a private telegram to Hamilton seeking his approval to the nomination of Gooroodas Banerjee, a former Vice-Chancellor of the Calcutta University and now a prominent judge of the Calcutta High Court.[64] In their job of collection of evidence from ''the disgruntled M.A.s. and B.A.s'', the permanent members of the Commission were to be assisted by five local commissioners—Ashutosh Mukhopadhyaya for Bengal, Sankaran Nair for Madras, Chandavarkar for Bombay and Lewis and Bell for North Western Provinces and the Punjab respectively.[65] While announcing the appointment of the Indian Universities Commission, Curzon also made an appointment to the newly created post of the Director-General of Education discussed at the conference at Simla and later approved by Hamilton. Orange who had two first classes from Winchester and Oxford and was then working in the Department of Education as an Examiner in the White Hall was appointed to the post on the recommenda-tion of Sadler[66] who was first offered the post but declined to accept it.[67]

The Indian Universities Commission started its work at Madras on 18 February and after examining 156 witnesses including only 63 Indians at different places, the Commission submitted its recommendations on 9 June to Curzon who in a delightful mood wrote to Northbrook, ''My Universities Commission has just reported.''[68] It is not necessary to enter here into details about the various recommendations of the Commission nor Gooroodas Banerjee's disagreement with them in his *Note of Dissent* as the Commissions recommendations faithfully reflected Curzon's views on the reform of the Indian University first elaborately delineated in his minute on 23 February 1901 and later discussed and endorsed at the conference at Simla. What is interesting to note here is the Commission's views on legislation to imple-ment the changes suggested by its recommendations. The Commission felt since the changes did not ''involve repeal of the existing Acts of Incorporation'' the Legislature could ''give effect to our proposal by passing a general Indian University Act, which would be construed as supplementing and amending the Acts of Incorporation.''[69]

Curzon never wanted to make the recommendations of the Indian Universities Commission public just as he had earlier prevented the proceedings of the Conference at Simla from becoming public. However, a local newspaper got hold of a copy of the report ''probably through the agency of some clerk'' and began ''publishing a series of daily denunciations of the Government or rather of myself, for having rung the death-knell of higher education in India.''[70] ''You are certain to be attacked'', consoled Hamilton,

> ''if you attempt to in any way purify university education and to free it from its existing excrescences. The Babu believes that one of the main objects for which British Rule was established in India was to enable him to get university degree; and any attempt to heighten the standard is sure to meet with violent abuse. But I have been so long the subject of almost universal abuse and misrepresentation by the Indian press, that I am compelled to attach little importance to what they say.''[71]

A fortnight after Hamilton had despatched his letter to Curzon from London, Curzon wrote to Sir Henry Cotton on 31 August, ''The Bengalis are denouncing me like fury because the University Commission has reported in a sense that they dislike. They seem to think that I both dominated the enquiry and wrote the Report. What a strange people! They take the heart of one.''[72] Ten days later, he wrote to Hamilton, ''the Town Hall and the Senate Hall of the university have been packed with shouting and perspiring graduates, and my name has been loudly hissed as the author of the doom of higher education.''[73]

Curzon psychologically reacted to the ''fierce agitation'' as he described it in one of his letters to Hamilton, put up by the Indians not only in Bengal, but also in Bombay and Madras and decided to consult the local governments before drafting the Indian Universities Bill based on the recommendations of the Commission. As there had been not much differences in the views offered by them, he went ahead with the drafting of the Indian Universities Bill.[74] At the same time he asked Ibbetson, Risley and Orange to help him prepare a State Paper on education ''to assuage the ill-feeling that may be aroused in some quarters by the Universities Bill, and that the public may be more inclined to accept reforms which are shown to be part of a great scheme, conceived on liberal principles and directed towards raising the standard of every aspect of education.''[75] In the same vein and acting on the same principle Curzon also added a provision to the Indian Universities Bill for financially assisting the Indian universities for a period of five years ''to gild as much as we can, that somewhat unpalatable pill that we are offering to the native patient, and the greater the generosity that we can show at the present juncture, the more likely are we to disarm antagonism, and to succeed.''[76]

The State Paper on Indian education was issued on 11 March 1904 and the Indian Universities Bill was passed despite stiff resistence at every passage of the Bill offered by G.K. Gokhale and Asutosh Mukhopadhyaya and became an Act on 21 March 1904 marking the end of ''a long and arduous struggle conducted for five years in the face of every discouragement and of bitter opposition.''[77] Two days after the Bill had been passed, Curzon, privately sent an indentical letter to the Governors of Bombay and Madras and the Lt. Governors of the North-Western Provinces and Bengal : ''The Universities Bill is now passed into Law; and the various Chancellors of the Universities will before long be called upon to take action under it.'' Next day he wrote to Godley in a very relaxed mood and heaving a sigh of great relief : "Here I have had the stiffest session on record, and have carried the Universities Bill, *which was my child.*"[79]

IV

Curzon's university reform represents a climax in the official attitude against the spread of higher education which had been developing ever since the mid-fifties of the nineteenth century. This seems a paradox, for, we are too familiar with the efforts made by the English officials for the spread of higher education in the first half of the nineteenth century. By higher education here we mean Western education and though Charles Grant's ideas of introducing it in India to reform the Indian society of its various evils like sati, infanticide, purdah and polygamy as well as to bring the Indians and the English officials closer together were strongly resisted by the East India Company in 1793 partly because of its reluctance to interfere with the Indian society and partly because of the proneness of the age to subversion, they were successfully revived later by Maculay and the government order that followed Maculay's minute of February 1835 not only made English the official language in British India replacing Persian but also banned any further expenditure on Oriental education in future. The change in the situation could be explained partly by the ideas of utilitarianism carried by the young English officials to India and partly by the emergence of an enlightened body of Indians headed by Raja Ram Mohan Roy.[80] These young Indians saw in the introduction of English education an opportunity to employment in various British establishments, official as well as non-official, that were then emerging in metropolitan cities, Calcutta, Bombay and Madras as well as up country in British India. Though the officials of the East India Company, Writers and Cadets as they were then called, were always recruited in London, there was always the demand for local hands to assist them in the administration of the growing British establishments. The East India Company authorised the Indian administration to make local appointments for very lowly paid jobs and those young men who had a knowledge of the English language, not necessarily of the English literature always, came handy for such appointments. The number of colleges in the metropolitan cities of British India imparting Western education, many of which like the Hindu School of 1817 which became the Presidency College in 1853 when Dalhousie reformed it, grew out of schools teaching alphabet along with "Shakespeare, the Calculus, Smith's Wealth of Nations, and the Ramayana"[81] under the same roof was not large and so was the number of the students who attended them. Students taught in these colleges could easily be absorbed in the services of the East India Company and other British establishments. They were docile, submissive and active participants in the British administration and because of the opportunities offered by the English education, there was a great demand for it particularly in Bombay, Calcutta and Madras which led F.J. Mouat, Secretary to the Council of Education in Bengal to actually submit a plan for university education in India in 1845. These groups of Indians formed the nucleus of the Indian middle classes. They were not critics but admirers of the British administration. So when the revolt of the sepoys swept the Indian sky in 1857, they remained quiet and silent spectators to it. They had actually become a class of people very much after the vision of Macauly in 1835 : "a class of persons Indian in blood and colour, but English in taste, in opinions, in morals and intellect."

This situation started changing since the mid-fifties of the nineteenth century and the starting point of this change may be said to have been marked by the establishment of the three universities at Calcutta, Bombay and Madras in 1857. Henceforth colleges became an integral part of the university system in India and they could admit such students as had passed the entrance or matriculation examination held by the universities to which they were affiliated and impart instruction according to such courses only as had been prescribed by the universities. Contrary to Canning's expectation in 1857, that the universities in India would become "an aristocratic institution" which could be mainly attended by the children of "the nobility and upper classes of India", they became "popular institution"[82] attended largely by the children of the new middle classes that had been emerging ever since the beginning of the nineteenth century. Because of the material advantages of holding university degrees, a very large number of those who passed the matriculation sought admission to these universities. The number of colleges which was 27 in 1857 rose to 55 in 1873 and that of students rose from 219 in 1857 to 4,499 in 1873.[83] In 1881 the corresponding figures were 85 and 7,582 respectively.[84] The number of students who succeeded in their examinations in the years which followed the establishment of universities was also considerable. Between 1857 and 1873, for example, the number of successful candidates from matriculation onwards was 12,392 at Calcutta, 5,502 at Madras and 2,703 at Bombay.[85] The annual output of the recipients of the bachelors degree also increased with the growing years since 1857 and there were 175 graduates by 1870, 404 by 1880 and finally 470 by 1884.[86] Failures of the "First Arts" Examination in 1870 were 570, in 1880, 1,110 and in 1884, 1289.[87] The figures for the class of persons educated in English could be obtained by tallying for 1857 through 1884 the total number of successful candidates for 1857 for First Arts and B.A. diplomas and degrees and adding it to the successful final candidates. Henry Maine estimated five times 5,000 B.A., M.A. for 1853 through 1883 or 25,000 out of an estimated population of 250, 000, 000.[88]

Having received a good secondary school education upto the level of matriculation and having attended a university, these men were certainly very educated compared to the illiterate town-dwellers or village ryots. They themselves were very much aware of this difference. What was the prospect open to the large number of students who were thus able to receive higher education? For one thing, a career in the Indian Civil Service was virtually never open to talent, though the principle had been asserted time and again in the Charter Act of 1833 and the Queen's Proclamation of 1858 after the Mutiny. Some avenues like army and politics were closed altogether. In those days, agriculture offered no temptation to an educated person and neither did manufacturing and commerce for the latter were almost impossible without skill, capital and equality in terms of competition with European businessmen.

As a matter of fact, the very nature of the course with their ''unique and disproportionate attention'' to literature and philosophy, [89] compared with physical and cognate branches of practical instruction tended to limit the choice of a career to either the service of government or similar employment.[90] ''What else can he do but qualify himself'', lamented a Calcutta Newspaper,[91] ''or, if he is father, train his son for the public service or one of the learned professions?'' In theory, the convenanted civil service [92] was open to the Indians since 1853 but in practice difficulties stood in their way - the early upper age-limit for the examination, the content of the syllabus, the expense of going to London where the examination was held, the Hindu prejudice against crossing the '' blackwater'', and the official reluctance of the British to admit Indians into this vital service. The educated Indians could only avail themselves of the posts at the lower level of the uncovenanted service which continued to remain open to them. Here the salaries were very poor, prospects for promotions negligible and conditions of service very bad.[93]

Since men were not often employed outside their own provinces, less than two thousand posts were available in the unconvenanted executive and judicial branches in Bengal, Bombay and Madras, for the graduates of the universities in these areas. Not all of them were given to the educated; in Bombay and in Madras less than half of the uncovenanted civilians had qualifications in the new education while in the North Western Provinces and in the Punjab most of these posts went to those who could not boast of any qualifications at all.[94] The creation of nine departments of education by 1879 as per the provision of the Education Despatch of 1854 and the gradual development of a graded Indian educational service to man these departments and the colleges under them opened new vistas for employment in the British India—but the posts in this uncovenanted service were not normally open to the educated Indians but to the European with qualifications from British universities, particularly from Oxford and Cambridge. In the whole of British India while there were only five educated Indians serving this uncovenanted service, the number of Europeans serving it was 95 by 1879. [95]

The paucity of suitable openings in the public service naturally compelled many to turn to independent professions such as teaching, law, journalism and medicine. Unlike the government servants who were inhibited by their dependence on the goodwill of the government which employed them, in these professions they had greater opportunity to take part in public life. By the end of the 1870s, there was hardly any important town in India which did not possess a sprinkling of teachers, lawyers, journalists and physicians who took a very lively interest in the social, political, economical and religious questions of the day. [96] It was this group of people who later formed the backbone of the Indian National Congress and because of their complaints against the government they were often distrusted and ridiculed by the European officials and the English press.[97]

It is thus obvious that the moderate difficulties of the

1850s in finding a suitable employment by the educated Indians, had become a major problem in the 1870s. A year before the establishment of the universities in India, *The Friend of India*, had warned of the problem : "Native education had gone so far that it has become one of the most serious problems of the day. What to do with our educated men."[98] Since 1857 when the higher education in India started expanding by leaps and bounds, the problem also became aggravated. By 1877 it reached such dimensions that Sir Richard Temple, the Lieutenant Governor of Bengal, did not hesitate to record a minute on it :

> "It is melancholy to see young men, who once appeared to receive their honours in the university convocation now applying for some lowly-paid appointment, almost begging from office to office, from department to department, or struggling for the practice of petty Practitioner, and after all this returning baffled and disheartened to a poverty stricken home, and then to reflect how far happier their lot might have been had they, while at school or college, been able to move in a healthier atmosphere of thought and freer walks of life. Nevertheless, perhaps thousands of young men persist in embarking on the same course, which can lead only to the same sad ending."[99]

The incidence of unemployment among the educated Indians made them discontended with the *British Raj* which not only gave them no relief or sympathy but even excluded them from higher posts in the army, education and the civil service. They saw the grand spectacle of thousands of foreigners being given precedence in appointments to all the best places under the administration. In the press and on the platform, the professionals joined the educated unemployed in waging an acrimonious war of criticism on the Government of India as responsible for the prevailing unemployment. The attack against the government was on two grounds; first, the system of education provided by the government and second, its failure to employ those who had been trained by it. In 1882, the very year which saw the appointment of an education commission, Dadabhai Naoroji, wrote to the Secretary of State for India on the subject of unemployment among the educated Indians :

> "The thousands that are being sent out by the universities every year find themselves in a most anomalous position. There is no place for them in their motherland. They may beg in the streets, or break stones in roads for aught the rulers seem to care for their natural rights, position and duties in their own country. They may perish or do what they like or can, but scores of Europeans must go from this country to take up what belongs to them, and that in spite of every profession for years and years past and upto the present day, of English statesman, that they must govern India for India's good, by the words of the august Sovereign herself."[100]

Next year, the contributor to the *Indian Spectator* brought out more clearly the difference between the prospect of an educated Indian and that of an Englishman :

> "How many university graduates go without work? The luckiest of them is often too glad to begin life as a *Mamlatdar's* [101] clerk. Now look at his English contemporary. The very first appointment he holds is that of Assistant Judge or Collector. What a difference when both had worked equally hard! The native graduate knows his importance, he feels his neglect all the more bitterly. He has the power to do harm, and may exercise that power. The uneducated does not feel neglect, he can get some work or other which he is not too proud. Not so that educated youth. He knows his marketable value and when neglected, he frets and fumes."[102]

Such criticisms were likely to arouse the suspicions of the Government of India, the provincial authorities and the British press. As the *Englishman* wrote in 1870 :

"The number of thinly veneered, but highly polished, students who are every year turned adrift into the world from our Anglo-Indian schools and colleges is perfectly appalling. Puffed up with a motion of superiority to the rest of their countrymen, they are no longer content to apply themselves to the industrial pursuits of their forefathers but demand employments more suited to the educational aroma with which they are imbued. Failing this, they spread abroad over the land, diffusing a feeling of discontent wherever they settle down, and stirring up disaffection to the very Government whose fond weakness has given them whatever strength they possess."[103]

In the same year that the *Englishman* made these comments, official scepticism about the value of the spread of higher education began. It was presumably provoked by the fact that in 1869 three Indians had successfully competed in the civil service examination.[104] If more money were spent on higher education, many more Indians would be able to enter the civil service, hitherto a European preserve. In May 1870 the *Supplement* to the *Gazetteer of India* carried a resolution by the Government of India in the Finance Department, dated 31 March 1870 after having referred to the resolution of 8 September 1869 which spoke about the withdrawal of the financial assistance by the State for the instruction of the people of Bengal in the English language; the resolution of 31 March 1870 went further to declare that the motives which induced the people to seek instruction in the English language were *prima facie* sufficient for its rapid development without any contribution from the Imperial finances whereas the desire for vernacular education required much artificial stimulus and encouragement. Therefore, "it should be, in accordance with the views expressed by successive Secretaries of State, the constant aim of the Supreme and the Local Governments...to reduce to the utmost the charge upon the state of English education in the view of rendering it as self-supporting as possible."[105]

The publication of this resolution was the signal for an agitation in Bengal which was unprecedented in intensity and magnitude. Without government assistance most of the Indian high schools and colleges which mostly drew their students from the middle and lower income groups and depended for their existence on the grants-in-aid system, would have to close down. The Bengali press raised the cry of "higher education in danger" and in view of the agitation carried out by the British Indian Association at Calcutta and in the mofussil, the government withdrew the resolution and assured the public by denying that it had any intention of stopping its assistance to higher education. All the while, the English-language press owned and managed by the Europeans, severely criticised the government's policy of supporting higher education. It pointed to the existence of a reaction against it among the Englishmen in India and in Great Britain including those who had earlier supported the spread of English education in India. The press openly said that the time would soon come when the Government of India would have to revise its policy respecting the education in English for Indians.

However, that time for the revision of its policy towards English education did not come until the end of the 1870s when movement in many parts of India grew up about the reduction from 21 to 19 the maximum age at which the Indian civil service examination could be taken by the candidates. This lowering of the age-limit by Lord Salisbury in 1876 was primarily aimed to make it more difficult for Indians to come and compete at London. As early as 1866, educated Indians had opposed the reduction of the maximum age limit from 22 to 21 because they thought it was injurious to Indian aspirants; the further reducation from 21 to 19 was even more unacceptable to them. They looked upon it as a manoeuvre on the part of the Government of India. to thwart the ambition of Indians to enter the civil service. Under the leadership of Surendra Nath Banerjea, they decided to organise a national protest which would invoke the Charter Act of 1853 and the Queen's Proclamation of 1858 in which the rights of the Indians for service in the administration, irrespective of class, creed, caste and colour had been proclaimed. On 24 March 1877, a public meeting was held at the Albert Hall, Calcutta, and a committee consisting of the representative of educated sections of the Indian community in Calcutta was appointed to draw up a memorial drawing attention to the principles and pledges contained in the Charter Act of 1833 and the Queen's Proclamation of 1858 and to forward it to Parliament. Surendra Nath Banerjea was assigned the task of travelling all over the country in order to gain support for the memorial. In April 1879, Lal Mohan Ghose was asked by the Indian Association to go to Great Britain as its representative to lay before the British public the grievances of the Indian people regarding access to appointments in the civil service and other questions as well. [106] This agitation which was supported by educated Indians throughout the country was organised and conducted with such care and in such a constitutional manner that it drew admiration from the Europeans also. "The really remarkable feature of the whole movement", wrote the *Times of India* on 24 December 1877, "is the moderation, the good sense, and political tact which have distinguished it from first to last...A race that can conduct a political campaign with such ability has already won half the battle."[107] The option and gradual extension of Western methods of agitation and organisation acquired through universities by the educated Indians posed a "real danger to our rule in India", as Hamilton pointed out decades later to Curzon.[108]

The commotion in Indian public opinion gave pause to the Government of India and induced it to consider the revision of its policy towards the education of Indians in the present system. "The present system", wrote the Rev. James Johnston in *Our Educational Policy in India* in 1880, "is raising a number of discontented and disloyal subjects."[109] Against this battleground, a liberal Viceroy, Lord Ripon took the most bold step of appointing the first education commission in 1882—called the Hunter Commission—to review the whole field of primary and secondary education in India. Its president—Sir William Hunter, thought that the governmentally supported education was producing a revolt among the educated Indians against three principles which represented "the deepest wants of human nature—the principle of contentment."[110] On the recommendations of the Commission, the Government of India, withdrew from activity in higher education, nominally as a measure of economy and it encouraged private enterprise in the field. It directed the local governments to close down or hand over to "a suitable agency, public or private", control over some of the mofussil government colleges while deciding to continue financially supporting the Presidency colleges "on which the higher education of the country mainly depends."[111] A stronger reason for the withdrawal was more political than economic. Lord Ripon in his convocation address at the University of Bombay in 1884 intimated—rather sympathetically to the Indian cause: "...that it is little short of folly that we should throw open to increasing numbers of the rich stores of Western learning; that we should inspire them with European ideas, and bring them into the closest contact with English thought, and that then we should as it were, pay no heed to the growth of those aspirations which we have ourselves created, and the pride of those ambitions we have ourselves called forth."[112]

However, as the Government of India diminished its role in higher education, Indians became more active; higher education instead of declining went on expanding every year. In 1881, for example, the number of colleges was 85, in 1886 it became 110 and in 1893 it rose to 156. Similarly, the number of students in these colleges rose from 7,582 in 1881 to 10,538 in 1886 and 18,571 in 1893.[113] Thus, within that decade following the withdrawal of governmental support for higher education, the number of colleges almost doubled, that of college students nearly trebled. The number of secondary schools also rose but not to the same extent. It rose, for example, from 4,122 in 1881 to 5,097 in 1893, i.e., nearly 25 percent in twelve years, while the number of secondary schools students, increased from 222,000 to 511,000 during the same period.[114] Within this same period, despite the desire of the Government of India to reduce its role in higher education, a university was established at Lahore in 1882 and the other at Allahabad in 1887 though obviously to reduce the burden on the Calcutta University but mainly because of the demand of these places for more higher education including Oriental.

The expansion of higher education in India in the decades following the report of the Hunter Commission was accompanied by an aggravation of the problem of unemployment among Indians educated in English. A district officer in Bihar suggested in 1882 that establishment of technical schools could alleviate unemployment and the consequent discontent : ''Unless technical schools are provided as outlets, the mere scholastic element will breed political discontent.''[115] In any case, the senior technical and jute mills, coal mines and iron foundries were recruited from Great Britain; the government, therefore, did not anticipate any improvement in the near future. There would have to be a long period of industrial development before there could be any opportunities for the employment of Indians with technical training. In a resolution of 18 June 1888 the government declared: ''In India at the present time the application of capital to industry has not been developed to the extent which in European countries has rendered the establishment of technical schools on a large scale an essential requisite of success. But the extension of railways, the introduction of mills and factories, the expansion of external trade and the large intercourse with foreign markets, ought in time to lead to the same results in India as in other countries, and create a demand for skilled labour and for educated foremen, supervisors and managers. It may be conceded that the effect of these various influences on an Asiatic people is very gradual, and that it would be premature to establish technical schools on such a scale as in European countries and thereby aggravate the present difficulties by adding to the educated unemployed a new class of professional men for whom here is no commercial demand."[116] In January 1889, Lord Lansdowne drew attention to the problem of unemployment when he addressed the University of Calcutta as it Chancellor:

"I am afraid we must not disguise from ourselves that if our schools and colleges continue to educate the youth of India at the present rate, we are likely to hear even more than we do at present of the complaint that we are turning out every year an increasing number of young men whom we have provided with an intellectual equipment admirable in itself but practically useless to them on account of the small number of openings which the professions afford for gentlemen who have received this kind of education."[117]

The growing unemployment among young Indians who had been educated in English and their disaffection for the Government of India which they held responsible for their plight, intensified nationalistic sentiments. They developed a collective consciousness of themselves, feeling solidarity with each other by reference to their common plight and the common objects of their grievance, they began to write letters to English dailies and to meet in associations to demand rights for educated Indians, especially those of representation and employment.[118] In 1885, when the Indian National Congress, which Hume saw as a safety valve to the growing discontent with the alien rule, was formed, it adopted "wider employment of our people in the public service", as one of "the three important questions" constituting "the chief planks in the Congress platform."[119] Hardly any annual session of the Indian National Congress took place without discussing the subject of the employment of Indians educated in English and passing resolutions on it.[120] In 1885, at the first session of the Indian National Congress at Bombay, Dadabhai Naoroji speaking in support of the fourth resolution of the Congress holding simultaneous examinations of the civil service in England and in India in accordance with the views of the India Office Committee of 1860 observed: "It is the most important key to our material and moral advancement. All our political reforms will benefit us but very little indeed if this reform of all reforms is not made. It is the question of poverty or prosperity. It is the question of life and death to India. It is the question of questions."[121] The Aitchison Commission which met next year to report on the state of the public services in India rejected the demand for simultaneous examinations in England and India for the Indian Civil Service but it proposed a scheme for doing "full justice to the claims of natives of India for higher employment in the public service." It recommended that the Indian Civil Service should be *corps d' elite* with its numbers limited to what was necessary to fill the chief administrative appointments of the Government of India and by transferring a corresponding number of appointments to local governments which were to be separately recruited in each province. The latter service, known as the Provincial Civil Service, should include 108 posts hitherto reserved for the Indian Civil Service and also the higher posts held by the unconvenanted service, which the Commission now abolished. The lower posts of the former uncovenanted service were, however, to be relegated to a Subordinate Civil Service.[122]

In 1889, 56 percent of the total appointments which numbered 25,370 and which were paid salaries of at last Rs.75 a month were held by the Indians, while only 14 percent of the appointments carrying salaries of Rs. 1,000 upwards "fall to our lot", said Surendra Nath Banerjea in commenting on these statistics, "although the country is ours, the money is ours and the bulk of the population is ours."[123] At the 16th meeting of the Indian National Congress in 1900, Surendra Nath Banerjea quoted figures for Bengal to show how the Government of India was not acting consistently with the various pledges and principles made in the Charter Act to 1833 and the Queen's Proclamation of 1858 regarding the employment of Indian's in the public service. He pointed out that the Indian's share in the higher grades in the Survey and Customs Department, Forest Department and the Postal Department was nil, while out of the 77 appointments in the higher grades in the Opium Department only 8, 2, 4, and 5 were held by the Indians respectively. "If you look at the statistics connected with these Departments", Banerjea observed :

"You will find that the higher offices, the bulk of the higher offices—I should not be guilty of the smallest exaggeration if I say that at least 90 percent of the higher offices—are filled by Europeans and Anglo-Indians...Imperialists, somebody says. They may be Imperialists or not but at any rate, these Departments constitute the close preserve, the absolute monopoly of these gentlemen. We are excluded. And why? Because of our race, our colour is our disqualification."[124]

While the "discontended B.A.s and M.A.s" must have shared Banerjea's views of the appointment of Indians to the Indian Civil Service and lesser services, some of them were becoming advocates of a more militant nationalism. The latter became adherents of the new generation of leaders like B.G. Tilak, Lajpat Rai and Bepin Chandra Pal, more "extremist" than the previous leadership. In Bengal, the extremist challenge began with Aurobindo's fierce attack on the Congress in 1893.[125] Next year, Alfred Croft reported in his Convocation Address at Calcutta in 1894 that lack of any suitable openings for those who had just been able to take their degrees as well as those who had failed was posing a grave problem. Quoting from Bacon's *Of Seditions and Troubles,* he underlined the danger by warning that one of the chief causes of discontent was "when more are bred scholars that preferment can take off."[126] In 1897, in the last year of Lord Elgin's viceroyalty when Bombay was threatened with an outbreak of plague, two educated young men, Damodar and Balkrishna Chapekar murdered Rand, the Collector and Plague Officer of Poona and his associate, Lt. Ayerst. As a reaction to the Poona murders, in 1898, the Government of India enacted the "Sedition Law"[127] After going through the papers leading to the Poona murders, Hamilton found it impossible to dissociate these young men's idea and hatred of England from the course of education and training through which they had passed.[128] Hamilton and his advisers regarded the Ferguson College at Poona where Damodar and Balkrishna had studied as the mainspring of a small but deep rooted political conspiracy in the Deccan.[129]

Hamilton's views on the Poona murders thus brought to a head the sentiments of those British officials who had since the early 1870s been pondering over the utility of spreading English education in India. Gustave LeBon, a French publicist and social scientist, who visited India in the early 1880s commented that English education was not at all suitable for the Indians who had a strong traditional culture. The latter could not satisfy the wants created by the English education and so the English educated wrote to the Indian press with bitter attacks on the *Raj*. The "Babus", as he called the English-educated Indians in Bengal, were the enemies of British rule and it was silly to rule the country through them : "Le pire ennemi de I' Angleterre placé sure le trone des Indes n' aurait pas porté a la metropole un plus grave préjudice"[130] In the decades following the birth of the Indian National Congress, it began to be thought that the decision to promote education in English, ever since the days of Macaulay, was a "short story of grave political miscalculation" containing a lesson "that has its significance for other nations which have undertaken a similar enterprise."[131] English education which was identified with higher education in India had given birth to a tone of mind and to a type of character that was "ill-regulated, averse from discipline, discontented, and in some cases actually disloyal." In short, it had raised "a fighting cock" while it was expected to raise "an innocuous hen". As Curzon later declared in connection with his scheme for education reform at the conference at Simla : "When Erasmus was reproached with having laid the egg from which came forth the Reformation, 'Yes', he replied : 'but I laid a hen's egg, and Luther had hatched a fighting cock'. This, I believe, is pretty much the view of a good many critics of English education in India."[132]

Curzon himself fully subscribed to this view. Five weeks after landing at Calcutta, while delivering the Calcutta University Convocation Address as its Chancellor on 11 February 1899, he observed that he knew, "that our system of higher education in India is a failure; that it has sacrificed the formation of character upon the alter of cram; and *that the Indian University turn out only a discontented horde of office seekers, whom we have educated for places which are not in existence for them to fill.*"[133] Since it was now too late to undo Macauly's or Bentinck's decisions to offer English education in India, the best could be done at the moment was to devise means to restrict its disadvantages. One of the means could have been to divert the attention of the young Indians from Western education to Oriental education which Annie Besant's Hindu College in Benares proposed to impart now "by undertaking the task of giving religious and moral education on Hindu lines to its youths."[134] Hamilton was willing to "encourage" Besant's scheme of education. As he wrote to Curzon in connection with Besant's Hindu College, "I think the real danger to our rule in India, not now but say 50 years hence, is the gradual adoption and extension of Western agitation and organisation; and if we could break the Hindu party into two sections holding widely different views, we should, by such a division, strengthen our position against the subtle and continuous attack which the spread of education make upon our present system of Government."[135] Another means would be, as had been unsuccessfully done by the government before in the 1870s and in 1882, to give more attention to education at the lower levels and less to higher education. Anything, Hamilton remarked rather gloomily, would be better than expansion of purely literary education, "joy of the Babu and anglicised Brahmin" which "produces a wholesale mass of discontented individuals who, if they cannot find government employment spend their time in abusing the government which has educated them."[136]

Curzon was not too happy with Besant's scheme because it was associated with "not merely active, but disloyal politicians" though Besant "herself had no political motives"; [137] he thought, however, that the best course to slow down what Hamilton later described in his *Reminiscenes* as the "educational juggernaut"[138] was to bring higher education under effective governmental control.[139] As we have already seen in the preceding section, this was exactly what was done by Curzon when he carried through the Indian Universities Act in March 1904 and that his plan to effect this reform through "legislation" after appointing "a small preliminary commission" had been disclosed to Hamilton as early as August 1901 after he had allowed himself sufficient time to study the university question in India.

It is a pity that Curzon's university reform has never been studied in the context of the developments affecting the interests of the British Raj in the decades that immediately preceded it. This is not to say that the universities in India were free from defects and that they did not need any reform though one may feel like agreeing with the observation made by the Indian Universities Commission in one of its introductory paragraphs in the *Report* that ''we are not disposed to confirm the sweeping condemnation which has sometimes been passed upon our University system.''[140] They did need reform because as we have already seen[141] they suffered form the limitations of the University of London which acted as a model to them in 1857. In the perculiar Indian conditions such limitations assumed gigantic proportions as to invite attention of all those authorities directly concerned with the state of higher education in the country. So when in 1898 when a Royal Commission was appointed under Lord Davey and the London University became a teaching unversity after the recommedations of the Davey Commission had been approved by the British Parliament,[142] the question of modifying the character of the universities in India became a question of time.[143] It is indeed an interesting coincidence that the person appointed to head the Government of India immediately after the Royal Commission to report on the London University was a person very much concerned with university education. ''I will not conceal from you'' Curzon told the young graduates of the Calcutta University in his first Convocation Address on 11 February 1899 as its chancellor, ''that I am a University Man to the core of my being....I have been an undergraduate of a university, a Bachelor of Arts, a Master of Arts, a fellow of a college and a Member of Convocation. But a Chancellor I have never been until today.''[144] Unfortunately, ''the University Man'' in Curzon was completely dominated by ''the Political Man'' in his person and he manoeuvred the university reform in such a way as to give top priority to safeguarding British interests in India.

The Indian intelligentsia could easily see in his attempt to control higher education in the country an attempt to stop the development of those historical forces associated with the spread of Western education which had contributed to their progress. As Surendra Nath Banerjea observed in his Presidential Address at the Ahmedabad Session of the Indian National Congress on 23 December 1902 that higher education "lies at the root of all our progress. It is the mainspring, the motive power, the germinal source of all those forces which make for progress... It is English education which has overcome the barriers of race, religion, and language, has dissipated the prejudices and mis-understandings of ages and has created those unifying influences which find a living expression in this vast, this stupendous, this majestic organisation of the National Congress. Could this educated community submit to the curtailment of this boon...to the restriction of its beneficent area?"[145] It may be asked if the British administration felt towards the end of the nineteenth century that the universities in India were breeding "fighting cocks" as Curzon described the educated Indians at the Conference of Simla in September 1901, threatening British interests in India, why did they not abolish them altogether instead of attempting to bring them under government control? Here again abolition of the universities would have gone against their interests, for the British in India always needed a Bilgrami, a Khan, a Bose, a Bhandarkar[146] or host of petty officials trained through these universities to help them prop up their administration in the country.

Indeed, one of the specific objects for the "encouragement" of higher education in India as mentioned in the Education Despatch of 1854 addressed on 19 July 1854 to the Governor-General of India was "to supply you with servants to whose probity you may with increased confidence commit offices of trust.''[147] However, India being a colonial country the demand for such servants was obviously limited and when the supply steadily overtook the demand, there was discontent writ large on the faces of the educated Indians including those who had taken to independent professions like law, teaching and journalism most reluctantly under the unavoidable circumstances. In those days young persons in India like their present day counterparts were no more interested in higher education than as children they were interested in their own birthday parties.[148] It was natural for the educated unemployed as well as for those professionals who were not patronised by the British establishments to become increasingly alienated with the British *Raj*.

Such alienation, however, was not a peculiar phenomenon in India alone despite her colonial character in the late nineteenth century. In Russia, for example, spread of higher education accompanied by a lack of suitable job opportunities had increasingly made the young educated Russians alienated with the Tsarist *régime*. The case of Russia was repeatedly cited by the members of Curzon's Council while debating on the draft Universities Bill in 1903. In a minute on 23 July 1903, Edward Law observed that ''in India the University system must lead to the same class of results as in Russia though it will take some time before it shows any acute and violent forms.''[149] He suggested that the situation could be remedied ''by raising fees so that only richer classes could afford to send their sons to a university.''[150] E.R. Ellis, another member of the Council, who also saw a parallel between Russia and Bengal as far as higher education was concerned, fully agreed with Law that high fees could probably get rid of the ''riff-raff''.[151]

Law and Ellis were probably echoing the fears of one of the father figures of higher education in India expressed nearly fifty years ago about the problems that could accompany its unplanned expansion. In a letter to Dalhousie on 8 June 1854 Charles Wood, President of the Board of Control between 1853 and 1855 and Secretary of State of India, 1859-66, pointed out that he was unwilling to provide higher education for all since this would create a "discontented class unless they are employed" and would ultimately ruin the British prospects in India.[152] In a letter to Halliday, the Lieutenant-Governor of Bengal, on 24 July 1854, he further clarified his views about the spread of higher education in India : "I do not see the advantage of rearing up a number of highly educated gentlemen at the expense of the state whom you cannot employ, and who will naturally become depositories of discontent. If they choose to educate themselves, well and good but I am against providing our own future detractors and opponents and grumblers."[153]

By bringing higher education under effective government control through the Indian Universities Act of 1904, Curzon only tried to tackle the realities of the problem visualised by Wood nearly half a century ago.

REFERENCES

1. For details see Papers relating to the Act VIII of 1904 (Calcutta, 1904)

2. Telegram from the Bombay Governor to the Viceroy, 24 January 1905. *Curzon Papers.* Microfilm Reel No. II. Hereafter cited simply as "Reel". *(Curzon Papers* on microfilm in the National Archives of India, New Delhi).

3. *Proceedings of the Legislative Council,* 3 February 1905, Nos. 20-29, p.36.

4. Lamington to Curzon, 28 January 1905, Letter No. 77, *Curzon Papers,* Reel No. II.

5. Curzon to Brodrick, 3 February 1905, Letter No. 92, *Curzon Papers,* Reel No. 6

6. Act No. II of 1905. See Appendix in *Leg. A. Proceedings*, February 1905, Nos. 20-29, P. 63

7. *University of Calcutta Convocation Addresses* 3 Vols. (Calcutta, 1915) Vol. 3, P. 955

8. Ghosh, S.C. *Dalhousie in India, 1848-56* (Delhi, 1975), p. 28-29.

9. See *Papes connected with the establishment of universities in India*. (Calcutta, 1857) as well as Richey, J.A., ed., *Selections from Educational Records, Part II, 1840-59* (Calcutta, 1922), p. 408 et. seq.

10. Naik, J.P., ed., *Selections from Educational Records*, (Delhi, 1963), Vol. 2. pp. 319, 467.

11. Richey, J.A., *op.cit.*, pp. 372-73, paragraph 30 of the Education Despatch of 1854.

12. *Home Edn. A Progs.* December 1901, Nos. 122-29, p.20

13. *Home Edn. A Progs.*, November 1899, Nos. 25-27, para 39, p.74.

14. See *Papers connected with the establishment of universities in India*. (Calcutta, 1857)

15. Naik, J.P., ed., *op.cit.*, p. 463.

16. *Ibid.*, p. 317

17. *Home Edn. A Progs.*, December 1901, Nos. 122-29, p. 29

18. *Ibid.*, p. 21

19. *University of Calcutta Convocation Address,* 3 Vols. (Calcutta, 1914), Vol. 2, p. 633 et seq.

20. *Home Edn. A Progs.*, December 1901. Nos. 122-29, p. 21.

21. *Ibid.*, p.26.

22. Maclean to Curzon, 23 April 1900, Letter No. 182. *Curzon Papers,* Reel No. 8.

23. University of Calcutta, *Hundred Years of the University of Calcutta 1857-1956* (Calcutta, 1957), p. 82.

24. For details see R. Nathan, *Quinquennial Review of the Progress of Education, 1897-98 to 1901-02* (Calcutta, 1902).

25. *Home Edn. A Progs.* November 1899, Nos. 25-27, paras 41-45, pp. 80-85.

26. *Ibid.*, pp. 74-75.

27. *Report of the Calcutta University Commission, 1917-19*, 13 Vols. (Calcutta, 1919-20). Vol-1. pp. 59-60.

28. Godley to Curzon, 15 December 1899, Letter No. 74, *Curzon Papers*, Reel No. 1.
29. Curzon to Hamilton, 23 March 1899, Letter No. 12, *Curzon Papers*, Reel No. 1.
30. *Ibid.*
31. Curzon to Godley, 18 October 1899, Letter No. 48, *Curzon Papers* Reel No.1.
31.a Curzon to Maclean, 14 February 1900, Letter No.44, *Curzon Papers*, Reel No.8.
32. Godley to Curzon, 15 December 1899, Letter No. 74, *Curzon Papers*, Reel No. 1.
33. "It is 47 Years ago since I wrote for C.Wood the Education Despatch of 1854"—Northbook to Curzon, 12 December 1901, Letter No. 44, *Curzon Papers*, Reel No. 6, Also see Ghosh, S.C., "Dalhousie, Charles Wood and the Education Despatch of 1854" *History of Education,* IV (Summer, 1975), p.38.
34. *Home Edn. A Progs.*, November 1899, No. 26, pp. 133-36.
35. Raghunatha Rao, C.S., ed., *Notable Speeches of Lord Curzon* (Madras, 1905), p.240.
36. Curzon to Woodburn, 13 July 1900, letter No. 10, *Curzon Papers,* Reel No. 8.
37. Woodburn to Curzon, 24 July 1900, Letter No. 30, *Curzon Papers,* Reel No. 8
38. *Ibid.*
39. *Ibid.*
40. Curzon to Woodburn, 29 July 1900, Letter No. 43, *Curzon Papers,* Reel No.8.
41. *Home Edn. A Progs.,* December 1901, Nos. 122-29, p. 17.
42. Curzon to Godley, 29 August 1900, Letter No. 56, *Curzon Papers,* Reel No. 2.
43. *Home Edn. A Progs.,* December 1901, Nos. 122-29, p. 17.
44. Dawkins to Curzon, 5 October 1900, Letter No. 187a, *Curzon Papers,* Reel No. 6.
45. Curzon to Dawkins, 29 August 1900, Letter No. 143, *Curzon Papers,* Reel No. 6.
46. When Dalhousie left India in 1856 after eight years of strenuous work as the Governor-General, he was almost a cripple. See Ghosh, S.C., *op.cit.*, p. 143.

47. *Home Edn. A Progs.,* December 1901, Nos. 122-29, pp. 19-27.

48. *Ibid.,* p. 28.

49. Curzon to Godley, 1 May 1901, Letter No. 31, *Curzon Papers,* Reel No. 2. Also, Curzon to Woodbrun, 28 May 1901, Telegram No. 160, *Curzon Papers,* Reel No. 2

50. *Home Edn. A Progs.,* November 1901, Nos. 47-71, p.9.

51. Curzon to MacDonnell, 3 August 1901, Letter No. 34, *Curzon Papers,* Reel No.9.

52. Curzon To Hamilton, 28 August 1901, Letter No. 59, *Curzon Papers,* Reel No.2.

53. *Ibid.*

54. *Home Edn. A Progs.,* November 1901, Nos. 47-61, pp. 167-68.

55. *Ibid.*

56. Curzon to Hamilton, 11 September 1901, Letter No. 62, *Curzon Papers,* Reel No.2.

57. *Home Edn. A Progs.,* October 1901, No. 19, pp. 25-28.

58. Curzon to Dawkins, 16 November 1901, Letter No. 33, *Curzon Papers,* Reel No.7.

59. *Home Edn. A Progs.,* October 1901, No. 19, pp. 25-28.

60. Curzon to Dawkins, 16 November 1901, Letter No. 33, *Curzon Papers,* Reel No. 7.

61. *Home Edn. A Progs.,* January 1902, No. 139, p. 15.

62. J.P. Hewett was Curzon's Home Secretary; A Pedler was Director of Public Instruction for Bengal; A.G. Bourne was Acting Principal of the Madras Presidency College, the Rev. D. Mackiehan was Principal of the Bombay Wilson College; and Syed H. Bilgrami, better known as Nawab Imad-ul-Mulk, was a graduate of a British University.

63. Banerjea, S.N. *A Nation in Making* (Culcutta, 1925), p. 162.

64. Curzon to Hamilton, 7 February 1902, Telegram No. 91, *Curzon, Papers,* Reel No. 5.

65. *Homie Edn. A Porgs.* January 1902, No. 139, p. 15. Mukhopadhyaya was a member of the Bengal Legislative Council, Nair a practising lawyer at the Madras High Court, Chandavarkar a Judge at Bombay High Court and Lewis and Bell were both directors of public instruction for provinces they represented.

66. Hamilton to Curzon, 6 January 1902, Telegram No. 27, *Curzon Papers,* Reel No. 5.

67. Hamilton to Curzon, 11 November 1901, Telegram No. 378, *Curzon Papers,* Reel No. 5.

68. Curzon to Northbrook, 21 July 1902, Letter No. 103, *Curzon Papers,* Reel No. 7.

69. *Report of the Indian Universities Commission, 1902,* 2 Vols. (Simla, 1902), Vol. 1. p. 55 *et. seq.*

70. Curzon to Hamilton, 23 July 1902, Letter No. 57, *Curzon Papers,* Reel No. 3.

71. Hamilton to Curzon, 13 August 1902, Letter No. 70, *Curzon Papers,* Reel No. 3.

72. Curzon to Cotton, 31 August 1902, Letter No. 124, *Curzon Papers,* Reel No. 7.

73. Curzon to Hamilton, 10 September 1902, Letter No. 72, *Curzon Papers.,* Reel No. 3.

74. *Home Edn. A Progs.,* December 1903, Nos. 67-74, 77-80.

75. Curzon to Brodrick, 4 November 1903, Letter No. 83, *Curzon Papers,* Reel No. 4.

76. Curzon to Godley, 23 September 1903, Letter No. 69, *Curzon Papers.* Reel No.4.

77. Curzon to Brodrick, 5 April 1904, Letter No. 18, *Curzon Papers.* Reel No. 4.

78. *Curzon Papers,* Reel No. 11, Letter No. 15.

79. Curzon to Godley, 24 March 1904, Letter No. 16, *Curzon Papers,* Reel No. 4, *Italies are mine.*

80. Ghosh, S.C., "Formation of an Educational Policy of the British Raj between 1757 and 1857" in Frijhoff, W., ed., *The Supply of Schooling* (Paris, 1983), pp. 43-56.

81. *Report of the Indian Education Commission, 1881-82* (Calcutta, 1883), p. 18.

82. University of Calcutta, *op.cit.,* p. 127.

83. Appexdix M. Statement 3 in *Report of the Public Service Commission, 1886-87.* (Calcutta, 1888), p. 81.

84. *Ibid.*

85. *Ibid.*

86. *Ibid.*

87. *Ibid.,* Appendix M, Statement 4, p. 82.

88. J. Strachey, *India* (London, 1903). p. 187.

89. For details about the courses, see Richey, J.A., *op.cit.*, p. 371 *et. seq.*

90. Temple, Richard, *Men and Events of my time in India,* (London, 1882), pp. 432-3.

91. *Indian Mirror,* Calcutta, 13 February 1878.

92. For the origin of the elite service, see Ghosh, S.C., *The Social Condition of the British Community in Bengal, 1757-1800* (Leiden, 1971), Chapter II.

93. Misra, B.B., *The Central Administration of the East India Company* (London, 1959), p. 404 *et. seq.*

94. See Appendix I to the *Report of the Public Service Commission 1886-87,* pp. 51-55.

95. Naik, J.P. and Ghosh, S.C., eds., *Development of Educational Service 1859-79* (Delhi, 1976), pp. XXIX-XXX, 361-70.

96. Seal, Anil, *The Emergence of Indian Nationalism* (Cambridge, 1968), Ch. 3, pp. 114-130.

97. "Wretched pettifogger"—this is how the Bengali lawyers were described by the *Pioneer* in July 1888. See Narain, Prem, *Press and Politics in India* (Delhi, 1976), p. 196.

98. *Friend of India,* Calcutta, 11 December 1856.

99. Extract from the Minute by the Lieutenant-Governor of Bengal on 5 January 1877 in *Report on the Administration of Bengal, 1875-77,* (Calcutta, 1877), p. 59.

100. *Journal of the East India Association,* XIV, 1882, pp. 171-72.

101. Subordinate Collector, normally held by an Indian.

102. *Indian Spectator,* Bombay, 27 May 1883.

103. *Englishman,* Calcutta, 28 February 1870.

104. All the three were Bengalees, They were Ramesh Chandra Dutta, Bihari Lal Gupta and Surendra Nath Banerjea. See Bose, Joges C., *Surendra Nath Banerjea* (Dacca, 1939), p. 20 and O'Malley, L.S.S., *The Indian Civil Service* (London, 1931), pp. 204-210.

105. Supplement to the *Gazetteer of India,* 7 May 1870, pp. 715-17.

106. Banerjea, Surendra Nath, *A Nation in Making* (Calcutta, 1925), p. 40 *et seq.*

107. *The Times of India,* Bombay, 24 December 1877.

108. Hamilton to Curzon, 20 September 1899, *Hamilton Papers,* Reel No. 1 (*Hamilton Papers* on microfilm in the National Archives of India, New Delhi).

109. Johnston, James, *Our Educational Policy in India* (Edinburgh, 1880), introduction. Also quoted in University of Calcutta, *op.cit., p. 150.*

110. *Report of the Indian Education Commission, 1881-82* (Calcutta, 1883). Also quoted in Mukherjee, Haridas and Uma, *The Growth of Nationalism in India* (Calcutta, 1957). p. 125.

111. For details, see *Report of the Indian Education Commission, 1881-82* (Calcutta, 1883).

112. Quoted in University of Calcutta, *op.cit.,* p. 152.

113. In Bengal alone between 1882 and 1893, seven new colleges emerged including those set up by Ananda Mohan Bose (City College), Surendra Nath Banerjea (Ripon College) and Girischandra Bose (Bangabasi College). See Ghosh, J., *Higher Education in Bengal under British Rule* (Calcutta, 1926), p. 165.

114. The data for this information is collected from (a) *Report of the Hunter Commission*, Ch. IV, pp. 256-312; *(b) Quinquennial Review of the Progress of Education,* 1886 by A. Croft, pp. 136-60 and 161-194; 1887-88 to 1891-92 by A.M. Nash, pp.51-83 and 85-132 and 1892-93 to 1896-97 by J.S. Cotton, pp. 70-115 and 121-170; (c) *Statistical Abstracts relating to British India* from 1877-78 to 1886-87 and 1891-92 to 1900-01 (See Tables under Education); (d) *Statement exihibiting the Moral and Material Progress and Condition in India,* 1881-82, 1886-87, and 1893-94 (See under Education).

115. *Statement exihibiting the Moral and Material Progress and Condition of India, 1882-83,* p. 148.

116. See *Papers relating to Technical Education in India, 1886-1904* (Calcutta, 1904). Also quoted in Crane, R.I., ''Technical Education and Economic Development in India before World War I'' in Anderson, C.A. and Bowman, M.J. eds. *Education and Economic Development* (Chicago, 1966), pp. 167-68, 180-81.

117. *University of Calcutta Convocation Address,* Vol. 2, p. 579.

118. Briton, Martin, Jr. ''Lord Dufferin and the Indian National Congress, 1885-88'', *Journal of British Studies*, VII, (November, 1967), pp. 68-96.

119. See *Report of the Proceedings of the Sixteenth Indian National Congress* on 28 December 1900, p.59.

120. See *Proceedings of the Indian National Congress* between 1885 and 1899.

121. See *Report of the Proceedings of the First Indian National Congress* on 30 December 1885, p. 81.

122. See *Report of the Public Service Commission, 1886-87 (Calcutta, 1888) for detais.* Also Ghosh, S.C. "Indian Nationalism and the emergence of the Public Service Commission", in the *Union Public Service Commission Souvenir Volume,* (Delhi, 1976), p. 6.

123. In 1903 Curzon had ordered a survey of appointments for the period of 36 years from 1867 to 1903. Surendra Nath Banerjea made this comment at the Twentieth Indian National Congress Session at Bombay in 1904. See *Report,* pp. 63-64.

124. *Report of the Proceedings of the Sixteenth Indian National Congress* on 28 December 1900, pp. 61-62.

125. For details, see Tripathi, A., *The Extremist Challenge* (Calcutta, 1967).

126. *University of Calcutta Convocation Addresses,* Vol. 2, pp. 735-36.

127. R.C. Dutt in his Presidential Address at the Lucknow Congress on 27 December 1899 commented that by passing this law, *Raj* committed "the blunder of connecting sedition with the spread of education". See *Report* p. 10.

128. Hamilton to Curzon, 11 October 1899, *Hamilton Papers,* Reel *No. 1.*

129. Hamilton to Curzon, 10 August 1899, Hamilton Papers, Reel No. 1.

130. Le Bon, Gustave, *Les Civilisation de l' Inde* (Paris, 1887), pp. 707-712.

131. See Sir Alfred C. Lyall's Introduction to Valentine Chirol's *Indian Unrest* (London, 1910), p.xiii-xvi.

132. *Home Edn. A progs.* October 1901, No. 19, Appendix A. p. 12.

133. Raghunatha Rao, C.S., ed., *Notable Speeches of Lord Curzon* (Madras, 1905), pp. 98-99. Also *University of Calcutta Convocation Addresses,* Vol.3, pp. 841-47, *Italics are mine.*

134. Besant to Curzon, 17 January 1899, Letter No. 18, *Curzon Papers,* Reel No. 7.

135. Hamilton to Curzon, 20 September 1899, *Hamilton Papers,* Reel No.1.

136. Hamilton to Curzon, 13 August 1899, *Hamilton Papers,* Reel No.1 Also quoted in Dilks, David, *Curzon in India.* 2 Vols. (London, 1969-70). Vol. 1, p. 244.

137. Curzon to Hamilton, 30 August 1899, Letter No. 38, Reel No. 1.

138. Hamilton, G., *Parliamentary Reminiscences and Reflections*, 2 Vols. (London, 1916, 1924), Vol. 1, p. 278.

139. Hamilton to Curzon, 18 May 1899, *Hamilton Papers*, Reel No. 1.

140. *Report of the Indian Universities Commission, 1902* (Shimla, 1902), Part I, paragraph 17, p. 15.

141. See section II.

142. *University of Calcutta Convocation Address*, 3 Vols. (Calcutta, 1914), Vol.3, p. 938.

143. *Report of the Calcutta University Commission, 1917-19, 13 Vols.* (Calcutta, 1919-20), Vol.I, p. 65.

144. *University of Calcutta Convocation Address*, Vol. 3, pp. 841-47. Also Raghunatha Rao, C.S., *op.cit.*, pp. 98-99.

145. *See Report of the Proceedings of the Eighteen Indian National Congress at Ahmedabad* on 23 December 1902, pp. 18-20.

146. Syed Ahmad Khan, as founder of the Anglo-Muhammadan Oriental College at Aligarh out of which later grew the Aligarh Muslim University provided an antidote to the Congress Movement since 1885 while as we have already noticed Syed A. Bilgrami, Bepin Behari Bose and R.G. Bhandarkar supported Curzon's university reform.

147. Richey, J.A., ed., *Selections from Educational Records, Part-II, 1840-59* (Calcutta, 1922), paragraph 3, p. 365.

148. Curzon himself admitted in his inaugural address at the Simla Conferecne on 2 September 1901 that the students went to universities (colleges) "not to learn but to earn." Full text of Curzon's speech may be seen in *Home Edn. A Progs.*, October, 1901, No. 19, Appendix A. pp. 11-23.

149. See *Home Edn. A Progs.*, December 1903, Nos. 67-86.

150. *Ibid.*

151. See Minute of E.R. Ellis on 25 July 1903, *Home Edn. a Progs.*, December 1903, Nos. 67-86.

152. Wood to Dalhousie, 8 June 1854. *Dalhousie Papers*, 57, p. 2. *(Dalhousie Papers* at the Scottish Record Office, Edinburgh).

153. Wood to Halliday, 24 July 1854. *Wood Papers, India Board : Letter Book*, Vol. 4. *(Wood Papers* at the India Office Library, London). Also see Ghosh, S.C., "Dalhousie, Chalres Wood and the Education Despatch of 1854", *History of Education*, IV. Summer 1975, p. 42.

SELECT BIBLIOGRAPHY

I. PRIMARY AUTHORITIES

Manuscript Sources
(A) Private Papers

Bentinck Papers at the Department of Manuscripts, Nottingham University Library; Alexander Duff Papers at the National Library of Scotland, Edinburgh; Dalhousie Papers at the Scottish Record Office, Edinburgh; Charles Wood Papers at the India Office Library, London; Bentham Papers at the University College Library, London; Curzon Papers (on microfilm) in the National Archives of India, New Delhi; Hamilton Papers (on microfilm) in the National Archives of India, New Delhi.

(B) Records

Despatches to India and Bengal and letters received from India and Bengal were consulted at the India Office Library, London while Educational Proceedings of the Home Department as well as Proceedings of the Legislative Council were consulted at the National Archives of India, New Delhi.

Printed Sources
(A) News Papers, Periodicals and Journals

Contemporary newspapers, periodicals and journals consulted for the specific periods in India include: *Bengal Harkaru (Calcutta), Calcutta Christian Observer, Calcutta Review, Friend of India (Serampore), Indian News (London), Indian Spectator, Indian Mirror, En-*

glishman, *Gazette of India, Times of India, Journal of the East India Association, Amrita Bazar Patrika* and *The Statesman.*

(B) Proceedings of the Indian National Congress between 1885-1905 consulted at the Nehru Memorial Museum and Library, New Delhi.

(C) Official Papers and Reports

Parliamentary History and *Parliamentary* Papers (House of Commons) for the relevant periods; W.Adam's *Reports on the State of Education in Bengal in 1835 and 1838* ed. by A.Basu, Calcutta, 1941; *Selections from Educational Records of the Government of India, Part-I (1781-1839)* and *Part-II (1839-59)* edited by H.Sharp and J.Richey respectively, Calcutta, 1920 and 1922; *Papers connected with the establishment of Universities in India,* Calcutta, 1857; *Papers relating to the Act VIII of 1904.* Calcutta, 1904; *Indian Educational Policy, 11 March, 1904,* Calcutta, 1904; *Quinquennial Reviews of Education* since 1886-87 upto 1906-07; *Report of the Indian Education (Hunter) Commission, 1881-82, Calcutta,* 1883; *Report of the Public Service Commission, 1886-87,* Calcutta, 1888; *Report of the Indian Universities Commission, 1902,* Simla, 1902; *Report of the Calcutta University Commission, 1917-19,* Calcutta, 1919-20; *Moral and Material Progress and Conditions of India* and *Statistical Abstracts* for the relevant periods.

(D) Contemporary Memoires, Letters, Diaries, Pamphlets and other Historical Studies

Arnold, E., *The Marquis of Dalhousie's Administration of British India,* 2 Vols. London, 1862-5

Auber, P., *An Analysis of the Constitution of the East India Company.* London, 1826

Argyll, The Duke of, *India Under Dalhousie and Canning.* London, 1865.

Bain, A., *James Mill*. London, 1882.

Baird, J.G.A., ed., *Private Letters of the Marquess of Dalhousie*. Edinburgh, 1910

Banerjee, S.N. *Speeches,* 6 Vols. Calcutta, 1908.

Bowring, J.ed., *The Works of Jeremy Bentham,* 11 Vols. London, 1843.

Broughton, Lord, *Recollections of a Long Life,* 6 Vols. London, 1909-11.

Campbell, G., *Modern India,* London, 1852.

Chirol, V., *Indian Unrest*. London, 1910.

Collect, S.D.ed., *Life and Letters of Raja Ram Mohan Roy*. London, 1900.

Cotton, A., *Public Works in India*. London, 1859.

Grant, Chales, *Observations on the State of the Asiatic Society*. London, 1797.

Gokhale, G.K. *Speeches,* 3 Vols. Poona, 1962, 1966-67.

Halévy, Élie, *La Formation du Radicalisme Philosophique,* 3 Vols. Paris, 1901-04.

..........*Histoire du peuple Anglais au XIXe Sìecle,* 5 Vols. Paris, 1912-32.

Howell, A., *Education in British India*. Calcutta, 1872.

Hunter, W.W., *The Indian Empire.* London, 1882.

Johnston, James, *Our Education Policy in India*. Edinburgh, 1880.

Kaye, J.W., *The Administration of the East India Company*. London, 1853.

Kaye, J.W. and Malleson, G.B. *History of the Indian Mutiny of 1857-58,* 6 Vols. London, 1888-89.

Lee-Warner, W., *The Life of the Marquis of Dalhousie* 2 Vols. London, 1904.

LeBon, Gustave, *Les Civilisations de l'inde*. Paris, 1887

Mill, James, *History of British India,* 3 Vols. London, 1817.

Mill J.S., *Dissertations and Discussions,* 2 Vols. London, 1859.

.............,*Considerations on Representative Government.* London, 1861.

Monier Williams, M., *Modern India and the Indians.* London, 1879.

Prichard, T., *The Administration of India,* 2 Vols. London, 1869.

Raghunath Rao, C.S. ed., *Notable Speeches of Lord Curzon,* Madras, 1905.

Raleigh, T., *Lord Curzon in India.* London, 1906.

Temple, Richard, *Men and Events of my Time in India.* London, 1882.

Trevelyan, C.E., *On the Education of the People of India.* London, 1838.

Trotter, C.J., *Life of the Marquis of Dalhousie.* London, 1889.

University of Calcutta, Convocation Addresses, 1858-1914, 3 Vols. Calcutta, 1914.

West, A., *Recollections, 1832-86,* 2 Vols. London, 1899.

II SECONDARY AUTHORITIES

(A) Monographs

Anderson C. Arnold and Bowman, Mary Jean, eds., *Education and Economic Development.* Chicago, 1966.

Ballhatchet, Kenneth, *Social Policy and Social Change in Western India.* London, 1957.

Bearce, G.D. *British Attitudes Towards India.* Oxford, 1961.

Bose, Joges C., *Surendra nath Banerjea.* Dacca, 1939.

Briggs, Asa, *The Age of Improvement.* London, 1949.

Das, M.N., *Studies in the Economic and Social Development of Modern India.* Calcutta, 1959.

Embree, A.T., *Charles Grant and British Rule in India.* London, 1962.

Frijhoff, W., ed., *The Supply of Schooling.* Paris, 1983.

Ghosh, S.C., *The Social Condition of the British Community in Bengal.* Leiden, 1970.

Himmelfarlo, G., ed., *J.S. Mill's Essays on Politics and Culture,* New York, 1963.

Hundred Years of the University of Calcutta, Calcutta, 1957.

Maritn, Briton, Jr., *New India, 1885.* Bombay, 1969-70.

Mayhew, A., *The Education of India.* London, 1925.

McCully, B.T., *English Education and the Origins of Indian Nationalism.* New York, 1940.

Mehrotra, S.R., *The Emergence of the Indian National Congress.* Delhi, 1971.

Misra, B.B., *The Central Administration of the East India Company.* London, 1959.

Moore, R.J., *Sir Charles Wood's Indian Policy.* Manchester, 1966

Mukherjee, Haridas and Uma, *The Growth of Nationalism in India.* Calcutta, 1957.

Naik, J.P., and Ghosh, S.C., eds., *Development of Educational Service, 1859-79.* Delhi, 1976

O'Malley, L.S.S., *The Indian Civil Service.* London, 1931.

Philips, C.H., *The East India Company.* Manchester, 1940.

Rosselli, J., *Lord William Bentinck,* Delhi, 1974.

Stokes, Eric, *The English Utilitarians and India.* Oxford, 1959.

Seal, Anil, *The Emergence of Indian Nationalism,* Cambridge, 1968.

Shridharan, L.K., *Story of the Indian Telegraphs.* New Delhi, 1953.

Tripathi, A., *The Extremist Challenge.* Calcutta, 1967.

Young, G.M., ed., *Macaulay, Prose and Poetry.* London, 1967.

........., *Victorian England.* London, 1936.

(B) Learned Periodicals and Journals

Cambridge Historical Journal (London).

English Historical Review (London).

History of Education (London).

Minerva (London).

Modern Asian Studies (Cambridge).

St. Anthony's Papers on South Asian Affairs (London).

UPSC Souvenir Volume (Delhi).

Only relevant volumes of the above have been consulted.

(C) Theses and Dissertations.

Hjejle, Benedicte, ''The Social Policy of the East India Company with regard to Sati, Slavery, Thagi and Infanticide, 1772-1858.'' Oxford D. Phil. 1958.

Sen, K. ''Sir Charles Wood and the Origin and Evolution of Modern University Education in India during the Nineteenth Century.'' Sheffield M.A., 1960.

INDEX

Act of Incorporation, 79
　　1857, 75, 78
　　1882, 75
　　1887, 75
Agra College, 23
Aichison Commission, 104
Akbar, 13
Albert Hall, Calcutta, 100
Allahabad University, 72, 75
Anglicists, 23, 28
Anglo-Vernacular
　　apteducational epoch, 43
Anson, William, 83
Anti-British Sentiments, 11
Arnold, 13, 61, 62
Assam, 77
Auckland, 28
Ayerst, 106
Bacon, 106
Ballhatchet, K A, 25
Banerjee, Surandra Nath, 14,
　　100, 105, 110
Banerjee, Gooroodas, 88
Banerjee, Surendra Nath,
　　87-88
Bayley, 41

Beadon, 41
Bearce, Geroge D, 37
Bell, 88
Benares Sanskrit College, 26
Bengal, 19, 38, 77
　　Partition, 9, 14
Bentham, Henry, 10, 20
Bentham, Jeremy, 22, 53-54, 58,
　　61, 66
Bentinck, 9-11, 14-15, 17-18,
　　21-28, 64,107
Berry, 41
Besant, Annie, 107-108
Bilgrami, Syed, H., 87, 110
Birth of New India, 9-15
　　Curzon's University reform,
　　9
　　Stripping social evils, 10
Board Library, 39
Bombay University, 72, 75, 101
Bourne, A. G. 87
British raj in India, 65, 96
Brown, David, 18
Brunnow, 40
Burke, 82
Burma, 77

Buxar Battle, 18
Calculus, 92
Calcutta Madrassa, 23, 63
Calcutta University, 75, 78-79, 81-83
Cameron, C H, 38
Canning, 13, 74, 93
Caste ridden society, 13
Ceylon, 77
Chandavarkar, 88
Chapekar, Bal Krishna, 106
Charter Act in 1853, 11, 100
Child Marriage, 10
Church Missionaries, 41
Colville, 12, 41
Constantine, Grand-duke, 40
Cotton, Henry, 82, 89
Couper, 65
Croft, Alfred, 106
Curzon, George, 9-10, 13-14, 72-120
    Protest of educated Indians, 9 setup university by, 14
    University reforms, 13-15, 72-120
Dalhousie, 9-15, 33-36, 38-39, 41-48, 74, 85, 92
    Utilitarianism of, 53-71
Davey, 109
Davey Commission, 109
Dawkins, 84
Duff, Alexander, 26, 28
Duke of Argyll, 66
East India Co., 11-12, 18, 22, 91

Renewal of Charter, 20
East India House, 64
Edinburgh, 14
Educational Conference at Simla, 85-89
Education despatch of 1854, 12, 15, 33-57, 74, 80, 82, 95, 110
Elgin, 106
Ellis, E R, 111
Elphinstone, 37, 40, 64-65
English
    As medium of instruction, 19-20, 24
    A official language, 10, 19, 24
    Persion replaced to, 17, 19, 26
English education in India, 11-12, 17-31
    Bentinck on, 21-29
    East India co officials anticipated, 18-21
    Macaulay's minute, 17-18, 20
European library, 11
European literature, 24
Evangelical theology, 54
Female education, 12
Female infanticide, 12
Ferguson college, Patna, 106
Fraser, 82
General Committee of Public Instruction, 22-28, 48
    Macaulay as President, 24
    opposition of, 23

Ghose, Lal Mohan, 100

Glenelg, 41

Godley, Arthur, 81-82, 90

Gokhale, G. K., 90

Grant, Charles, 18-21, 43, 91
  To civilise Indians by diffusing European civilisation, 20

Grote, 25, 64

Halliday, 43, 112

Hamilton, 82, 86-90, 100, 106, 108

Hewett, J P, 87

Hindoo railway station, 13

Hindu College at Calcutta, 23, 36, 163

Hindus, 12

Hobhouse, John, 40

House of Commons, 67

Home, David, 20, 104

Hunter, WW, 62, 101

Ibbetson, 90

India House, 39

India Office, 67

India Office Committee of 1860, 104

Indian civil service, 87, 94, 104-105

Indian National Congress, 14, 67, 104-105, 110

Indian Universities Act of 1904-05, 1, 72-75, 108, 112
  Preambles in 74-75

Indian Universities Commission, 88-90

Infanticide, 25

Johnston, James, 101

Jowett, 83

Kaye, John William, 62

Lahore University, 72, 75

Lajpat Rai, 106

Lansdowne, 76-77, 103

Law Commission, 59

Law, Edward, 111

Le Bon, Gustave, 106

Lee-Warner, W, 48, 81

Lewis, 88

London, 14

Luson, 82

Luther, 107

Macaulay's Minute 11, 17-18, 20, 24, 27-29
  Theme of 17-18

Macaulay, Thomas Babington, 10-11, 14, 20-21, 27-28, 37, 41, 54, 65, 91-92, 107
  English education in India, 11
  Law Member of Governor Generals Council, 18, 21, 24
  Renewal of East India Co. Charter, 20-21

Macaulay, Zachery, 20, 27

Mackichan, D, 87

Maclean, 83

Madras University, 72, 75

Malthus, 54

Marshman, James, 3d, 41-42

Martin, Briton, 9

Mayhew, Arthur, 25

Mayo, 62

Melbourne, 54

Metcalfe, Charles, 25

Mill, James, 10, 20, 22, 27, 37

Mill, John stuart, 22-23, 53-55, 61, 64, 68

Moor, 48

Moore, R J, 33, 38, 40

Mouat, F J, 37, 41, 92

Mukhopadhyaya, Ashutosh, 88, 90

Munro, 37, 65

Muslims, 12

Mutiny of 1857, 66, 68, 94

Nair, Sankaran, 88

Naoroji, Dadabhai, 97, 104

National convention of France, 5 5

Nilgiris, 27

Northbrook, 11, 34, 82, 88

Northcote, Stafford, 82

North Western province, 35, 55, 50

Nottingham, 14

Ootacamund, 27

Orange, 88, 90

Orientalists, 23

Oriental learning and Literature, 11

Pal, Bepin Chandra, 106

Palmerstone, 41

Patrate, 13

Patna, 57

Pedler, 87

Peel, 54

Persian language, 10, 19, 26

Pitts India Act of 1783, 40

Plassey battle, 18

Polygamy, 10

Postal system, 58, 59

Presidency college at Calcutte, 36, 92

Prinsep, 41

Provincial civil service, 104

Punjab, 12

Punjab university, 75-76

Queen's proclamation of 1858, 100, 105

Railway, 13, 55-58, 63-65

Railway codes, 60

Raleigh, 83-84, 87

Ramayana, 92

Rand, 106

Revolt of 1857, 11

Ricardo, 54

Ripon, 101

Risley, 90

Roy, Raja Ram Mohan, 21, 23, 91

Russia, 18

Sadler, 88

Sati, 10, 18, 25

Salisbury, 67, 99

Seditation Law, 106

Sen, Kamala, 106

Shakespeare, 92

Shastras, 13

Shiva, 13

Smith, 92

Social evils, 10, 19, 26

Social revolution, 12

Spear, T G P, 25

Strachey, J., 64

State Paper on Indian Education, 90

Stephen, James, 20

Stokes, Eric, 54, 61, 64

Subordinate civil service, 105

Taj, 63,-64

Telegraph, 58, 65

Temple, Richard, 96

Text book committee, 81

Thomason James, 34-36, 39

Thomason's system of vernacular education, 34-36, 140

Thronton, Henry, 20

Thugi, 25

Tilak, B G, 106

Tipoo Sahib, 13

Tory, 53

Trevelyan, Charles Ward, 11, 28, 38

Turnbull, George, 63

Udny, George, 18

University reforms by curzon, 9, 13-15, 72-120

    Academic degrees, 74-75

    Affective interest of British raj, 109-11

    Affiliating university, 79

    Affiliation of college to university, 73-74

    Appointment of professors and lecturers, 75

    Appointment to senates, 76

    Chancellor/Vice Chancellors, 73-74

    Choice of career, 94-96

    College System, 76

    Curzon's confrontation with Calcutta University, 81-83

    Defects of Act of Incorporation, 76

    Educational Conference at Simla, 85-87

    Education of undergraduates, 80

    Establishment of Universities, 92-93

    European Officials Connected, 75-76

    Expansion of higher education, 102-05, 112

    Failure of 107-08

    Governing Body of Senate, 78-79

    Higher education in danger, 99

    Indian public opinion, 101

    Indian Universities Act, 72-74, 89

    Indian Universities Commission, 88-91

    Legislation, 84-85

    Nomination right, 76

    Number of Colleges, 92-93, 102

    Official Septicism about higher education, 98-99

    Paucity in public service, 95

    Preambles in Act, 74

    Privilege of election, 77-78

    Proposal for reforms, 85

    Reduction in size of senates, 72

    Represents official attitude, 91

    Revision of policy, 99-100

    Secondary school education, 93-94, 102

    Spread of english education, 106-07, 110

Unemployment among educated Indians, 96-97, 104-04, 111

Vice-Chancellor, 83

Utilitarianism of Dalhousie, 53-71

Charter of, 54

How excercized to destroy prejudices and bring reforms, 55-58

Ideologically belonged to Bentham, 54

Interests of community in India, 64-65

Limitations of, 66

Material and moral progress of India, 65-67

Matefial improvement of India, 54-55, 62-63

Method, 61-62

Non-interference with religion of Indians, 63

Postal system, 58-59

Railway, 57-58

Railway codes, 60

Social improvements in India, 53

Suggestions to Council of education, 63

Uniformity of management, 59-60

Western innovations, 67-68

Vedas, 13

Widow remarriage, 12, 58

Wilberforce, William, 20

Williams, M Monier, 36

Woodbrun, 82-83

Wood, Charles, 11-12, 33-35, 37, 39-43, 47-49, 82, 112

Wood's education despatch, 12, 33-52

British attitude towards India, 37

Critical study of, 36-37

Dalhousie analysis of, 43-47

Establishment of University, 44-46

Grants-in-aid, 46-47

Dalhousie letter to Wood on, 39

Dalhousie Share in Composition, 33-34, 41-43

Lord's Committee on Education, 38

Marshman on, 38-39

Scheme of Modern Indian University outlined, 37

Stages in which passed, 35-36

Wood letter to Dalhousie on, 40

Wood letter to Elphinstone, 40

Young, G M, 54